SKYWALKING

SKYWALKING

☆ ☆ ☆ ☆ ☆ ☆ ☆ ☆ ☆ ☆

How Ten Young Basketball Stars Soared to the Pros

JEFF RUD

POLESTAR
BOOK PUBLISHERS

Polestar Book Publishers acknowledges the ongoing support of
The Canada Council; the British Columbia Ministry of Small
Business, Tourism and Culture through the BC Arts Council;
and the Government of Canada through the Book Publishing
Industry Development Program (BPIDP).

Cover design by Jim Brennan.
Cover photo of Vince Carter of the Toronto Raptors
  by CP Picture Archive (Kevin Frayer).
Author photo by Bruce Stotesbury, Victoria *Times-Colonist*.
Printed and bound in Canada.

Canadian Cataloguing in Publication Data
        Rud, Jeff, 1960-
        Skywalking
        ISBN 1-896095-46-1
        I. Basketball players — Biography.   2. National
Basketball Association — Biography. I. Title.
GV884.A1R82 1999   796.323'092'2 C99-910737-2

Library of Congress Catalogue Number: 99-64176

POLESTAR BOOK PUBLISHERS
P.O. Box 5238, Station B
Victoria, BC
Canada   V8R 6N4
http://mypage.direct.ca/p/polestar/

In the United States:
POLESTAR BOOK PUBLISHERS
1436 W. Randolph St.
Chicago, IL
USA   60607

03 02 01 00 99 • 5 4 3 2 1

The author would like to thank the following people and organizations for their time and co-operation in this project:

Polestar managing editor Lynn Henry; Polestar publisher Michelle Benjamin; Shareef Abdur-Rahim; William Abdur-Rahim; Doug Lipscomb; Vancouver Grizzlies media relations staff; Howard Tsumura, Vancouver *Province*; Ken Shields; Toronto Raptors media relations staff; Michelle Carter-Robinson; Charles Brinkerhoff; Bill Cole, *Winston-Salem Journal*; Wake Forest University athletics staff; Dave Odom; Tina Tobias; Minnesota Timberwolves media relations staff; Rob Babcock; University of Tennessee athletics staff; Mickie DeMoss; Bob Mackey; Craig Esherick; Georgetown University athletics staff; Steve Nash; John and Jean Nash; Ian Hyde-Lay; Dick Davey; Santa Clara University athletics staff; Tim Kawakami and Scott Howard-Cooper from the Los Angeles *Times*; Michael Olowokandi; Chris Ford; University of the Pacific athletics staff; Bob Thomason; Ron Verlin; Adam Jacobsen; Tony Marcopulos; Charlotte Hornets media relations staff; University of Virginia athletics staff; Dawn Staley; Debbie Ryan; and Rich Yankowitz.

A special thanks to Lana, Maggie and Matthew.

To my parents, who have always encouraged dreams, shared their wisdom, offered their support and, most importantly, provided their unconditional love.

SKYWALKING

INTRODUCTION

SKYWALK: To stay airborne, as if walking on air.

If you are a basketball fan, chances are you hold a vivid memory of the first time you laid eyes on a player who was capable of skywalking. Not simply jumping or scoring — all professional basketball players can do that — but skywalking: soaring and improvising and creating something wonderful out of the smallest sliver of opportunity.

My first such memory was given to me by my father in the fall of 1976, after we had moved from the Canadian prairies to San Antonio, Texas. A budding teenage basketball enthusiast, I eagerly hounded Dad to purchase a season-ticket package for San Antonio's inaugural campaign in the National Basketball Association. And from the very first night we set foot in HemisFair Arena, when I was spellbound by the majestic flights of spindly Spurs' star George (Iceman) Gervin, I knew I was hooked. I was an NBA fan for life.

It is out of this initial thrill that, 23 years later, *Skywalking* is born. Among these tales about ten of today's up-and-coming pros, there are certainly a handful of players who defy gravity with a rare and beautiful artistry. The obvious physical gifts of young stars such as Kobe Bryant, Vince Carter, Allen Iverson, Shareef

Abdur-Rahim and Chamique Holdsclaw are a big part of what we were thinking when we titled this book. Dig deeper than that, however, and you'll find that *Skywalking* is also about reaching for your dreams, no matter how impossible they might seem. Seven-footer Michael Olowokandi of England dared to reach across an ocean and his dream came true in spectacular fashion when he was chosen No. 1 overall in the 1998 NBA Draft. Point guard Steve Nash dared to dream, too, and wound up beating massive odds to become the highest-ranked Canadian hoopster ever selected. Kevin Garnett and Kobe Bryant dared to believe that they could jump straight from their high school proms into the planet's greatest basketball show; as a result, they became two of the NBA's hottest young commodities.

Skywalking is about great basketball talent, to be sure, but it's also about great stories. Like the story of Dawn Staley, who as a plucky North Philadelphia teenager ignored all the young men who would have shooed her from their pickup games and went on to become the consummate playmaker in the women's pro game of the 1990s. Like the tale of towering Tim Duncan, who went from unknown youngster on a tiny Caribbean island to NBA Finals MVP in just six short years. Or like Allen Iverson, who spent time in prison as a teenager but managed to pull his life and his basketball career back together and became the shortest scoring champion in NBA history.

Above all, *Skywalking* is a collection of athletes and people who are capable of taking your breath away, not only with their talents but with their determination.

For an awestruck kid in San Antonio back in the 1970s, the inspiration was the Iceman. For many youngsters of the new millennium, inspiration is in the players who grace these pages.

SHAREEF ABDUR-RAHIM

Skinny six-year-old Shareef Abdur-Rahim could barely contain his excitement as he bounded through the door of his family's Atlanta home. Clutched in the wide-eyed youngster's right hand was a flyer he had picked up at a local recreation centre. It advertised a community basketball league for children.

"Can I play? Can I play?" the grade-schooler breathlessly asked his father.

"You *really* want to do this?" the father asked his son slowly. "Can you take out the trash, rake the leaves, keep your grades up? If you can do all that, you can play."

William Abdur-Rahim was dutifully playing the disciplined dad, but inside he was secretly delighted. A former Georgia all-state basketball and football player in high school, he'd always hoped his children would follow in his footsteps, but he had never pushed a sport on any of them. Now his first-born son was asking for the opportunity.

Of course, it shouldn't have surprised anybody that Shareef Abdur-Rahim would gravitate toward a rim and a backboard. He and his sisters had been following their father to pickup basketball games for years, sitting and watching the men run up and down the court before running out onto the playing surface themselves.

"I really have to say, from that initial point of him asking if he could play, Shareef was dedicated to trying to be the best basketball player he could be," his father says now. "He worked hard, he was dedicated and he did what he was told." Part of that serious approach was the result of Shareef's deep love for the game of basketball and his corresponding desire to learn every possible thing he could about it. But another component of that unusual dedication was his upbringing. As a young man, William Abdur-Rahim had converted to the Islamic faith and he eventually committed his life to it by becoming an Imam, or religious leader, in Atlanta's Muslim community. His eldest son was brought up in strict but loving adherence to the Islamic tenets of submission to Allah, discipline, prayer, hard work, family values, good deeds and abstention from vice.

Shareef's early years were spent in the Muslim mosque education system, rather than the public schools of Atlanta. "That was a way of buffering him from the inner-city foolishness," his father says now. Like all devout Muslims, the Abdur-Rahims observed the month of Ramadan and, throughout the entire year, they prayed five times daily. It was Shareef's duty as the eldest son to call the family to the Fajr, or early-morning prayer, conducted between dawn and sunrise — sometimes as early as 5:30 a.m. Loosely translated into English, Shareef Abdur-Rahim's Muslim name means "noble servant of the most merciful one." Both he and his father will quickly tell you that Islam is not a religion to them, but rather a way of life. That way has helped to give Shareef the kind of self-discipline required to excel in the NBA. Even now, as one of pro basketball's rising young stars, he believes that basketball is something God has given him, and that if he misuses or disrespects that gift, it will be taken from him.

The home in which Abdur-Rahim grew up was middle-class and Shareef's mother, Aminah, was home to raise her children. But through the family's community charity work, Shareef also got a glimpse of how the less fortunate lived. He and his father together delivered food baskets to needy inner-city families and worked on an Atlanta project to rebuild run-down housing for the poor. Even as a child, this outlook deepened his appreciation for the good things he had in his own life. One of those good things was basketball. "I can remember my first year playing and scoring one point the whole year and having fun," Abdur-Rahim says, "and it probably being the most fun I've had playing basketball."

From that first dip into community league hoops, Shareef showed a determination to make the most of his opportunity on the court. The quiet, confident youngster dabbled in all sorts of sports, but it was evident early on that basketball was his first and fondest love. As a grade-schooler, he was tall and lanky, or, as his father remembers, "gawky." He also possessed plenty of natural talent and an unusual ability to absorb the lessons taught by his rec-league coaches. William Abdur-Rahim was one of those coaches, and he would guide his eldest son's team in Atlanta's community leagues for three seasons.

Shareef's early commitment to improving himself was by no means restricted to games, however. As a preteen, he would run hills with his father and he would practise his ball-handling and shooting for hours on end. "It was hard to get him off the court at night," his father recalls now. "He'd be shooting in the dark."

Young Abdur-Rahim didn't necessarily need a basketball, either. His father would sometimes put a mark several feet high on the outside of the house and ask his son to jump up and touch the mark 50 times before he went to bed. Within two or three weeks, Shareef would summon his father. "I'm doing it!" he would say. "Come, look, look, look!" Gradually the mark was raised, both literally and figuratively. By the time Shareef reached the seventh grade and switched to the public school system, he was being recruited by a number of Georgia high schools, as was his younger sister, Quadirha, a talented sprinter and basketball player. The family eventually settled on Wheeler High School in Marietta, Georgia, a suburb a few minutes outside Atlanta. Wheeler was a school of less than 2,000 students known more for its academics than its hoops history. The Abdur-Rahims decided it was the right place for Shareef and the rest of their children. The family relocated from Atlanta to Marietta. "Wheeler wasn't known as a basketball school back then," William Abdur-Rahim says. "But Wheeler is a basketball school now." This change is due in large part to a slender forward named Shareef.

It is unusual in Georgia high school hoops for a freshman to make the varsity team. But at six-foot-four and already possessing some undeniable skills, Shareef survived the final cut at Wheeler. That season, the Wildcats struggled to a 4–20 mark, but young Abdur-Rahim had already shown hints of what was ahead, including one memorable 17-point performance in a single half. The team's turnaround was in sight and he was leading the way.

Before Abdur-Rahim's sophomore season, a new head basketball coach arrived at Wheeler. The Wildcats improved dramatically under energetic young Doug Lipscomb, a former player at Middle Tennessee State who had previously been an assistant high school coach in Gainesville, Georgia. They finished the season at 15–12, reached the state final four and were named the turnaround team of Cobb County.

Meanwhile, the Wildcats' star was growing, both physically and in skill. His six-foot-six father had expected Shareef to be about the same height or slightly shorter and settle nicely into a role in the backcourt. But between February and October of his freshman and sophomore years, Shareef shot up to six-foot-seven and he didn't stop there. By the time he left Wheeler, he would stand six-foot-nine. And with Doug Lipscomb's help, his skill level rose along with his body. With plenty of extra individual attention that included spirited games of full-court one-on-one with Lipscomb, Shareef improved his ball-handling, jumpshot, co-ordination and agility. Soon Wheeler was blessed with a towering forward who was as quick as many guards, a player who could run the floor and finish with either an electrifying jam or a floating jumper. What's more, Lipscomb remembers his young star as an exceedingly nice kid, one who was extremely polite, one you could have felt comfortable leaving your own children with. "Shareef was very mature at a young age," says the coach.

"People say he has an old man's spirit in a young man's body," Shareef's mother, Aminah, once told the Vancouver *Sun*. As a young high school student, that unusual degree of maturity helped Shareef to weather the pain of his parents' divorce. It also helped him to realize that, although he was on his way to becoming a huge high school name, there was still plenty of room for improvement.

"Shareef's improvement in high school was due to hard work," Lipscomb says simply. "We have a program at Wheeler where we stress that. His attitude was one of 'refuse to lose.' It was old-school. He always wanted to play. He was always willing to work hard."

Although Abdur-Rahim is quietly confident by

nature, Lipscomb remembers his star becoming a vocal leader of the Wildcats as his high school career progressed. Often, the electrifying plays he was capable of making provided a special kind of leadership. And so did his desire to improve. "Shareef was by far and away our best player," Lipscomb says. "The rest of the kids worked hard and he was always there, working along with the other kids." That combination was enough to power Wheeler to its first-ever Georgia state 4A basketball title in Abdur-Rahim's junior year. The Wildcats beat Valdosta in the championship game played at Georgia Tech. To cap off a near-perfect prep season, Shareef averaged 31 points and 12 rebounds for the year and was named Georgia's Mr. Basketball.

It wasn't all smooth sailing, however. As Abdur-Rahim's reputation grew, so did the predictable resentment of some fans from rival schools. In particularly unenlightened gyms, opposing fans would chant "SAT, SAT, SAT," implying that Shareef lacked the intelligence to pass his college entrance exam (SAT or "Standard Aptitude Test"). "They assumed because he was big and black that he was dumb," Lipscomb would later tell the Vancouver *Sun*. "He was taught to overlook the bigotry and just keep drillin' those shots. Then our kids would answer back: 'NBA, NBA, NBA.'"

With Abdur-Rahim drilling those shots, Wheeler very nearly repeated as state champs in Shareef's senior year, a season in which students at the Marietta high school took to wearing T-shirts that read: "Shareef's House." The Wildcats again advanced to the state championship game, this time at Albany. They battled to the end against undefeated Dunwoody High, the No. 1-ranked team in Georgia, before being edged by two points in a high school heartbreaker. "It was one of those games where *they* made the shot at the end," Lipscomb says. "It's one of those games that you live with and you grow from."

Meanwhile, Shareef Abdur-Rahim had other things to consider. Following his stellar junior season, he had moved to the top of the list of nearly every college recruiter in the U.S. and a trip to Argentina with the American team for the world junior qualifying tournament further fuelled his reputation. During the 1994 Amateur Athletic Union (AAU) Junior Olympics in Florida, no less than 25 Division 1 NCAA coaches were on hand to watch Abdur-Rahim score 34 points in his first game. Everybody wanted this kid. "If you love basketball, you live for such moments — your first glimpse of a player you know you'll be seeing many more times," wrote Atlanta *Journal-Constitution* reporter Mark Bradley after seeing Abdur-Rahim play during his senior year at Wheeler. "No matter how famous they become, you still remember your first sighting of Isiah Thomas, of Darrell Griffith, of Wes Unseld ..."

As his high-school career was topped off by a second-straight Georgia Mr. Basketball award and a gaudy average of 32 points per game, there was no hotter college commodity than Shareef. The list of his college suitors was too long for anybody to remember. But in one week alone, North Carolina's Dean Smith, Georgetown's John Thompson, Duke's Mike Krzyzewski, and Georgia Tech's Bobby Cremins each paid a visit to the Abdur-Rahim household in Marietta. Ultimately, Shareef would reject all those high-profile suitors, choosing instead the University of California (or "Cal") at Berkeley. After a visit to the Bay Area campus, he told his parents he felt comfortable with the school, having seen students engaged in Islamic prayer on the campus lawns. He liked the Golden Bears' style of play under young coach Todd Bozeman, who was sensitive to Shareef's Islamic faith and would pay attention to the little details that would make him comfortable at Cal, like making sure his young star got turkey sausages, rather than pork, during road trips. In addition to feeling comfortable there, something about going to school in a new place was appealing to Abdur-Rahim.

If Cal appealed to Shareef, then Shareef certainly appealed to Cal. He would play only one season with the Bears, but it would be a memorable campaign that distinguished him as one of the finest freshman in NCAA history. Displaying a repertoire of silky-smooth spin moves and frightening quickness under the hoop, Abdur-Rahim led all freshmen in the nation in scoring at 21 points per game. He also established Cal freshman records for points (590), scoring average, field goals (206) and free-throws (170). Despite his first-year status, Shareef led the Bears in scoring, rebounding (8.4 per game) and steals (1.86 per game), and was second in blocks (1.25 per game).

His performance made him the first freshman in history to be named Player of the Year in the Pacific-10, a conference that has turned out a litany of basketball greats. Shareef was also one of 17 finalists for the John Wooden Award, given to the national collegiate player of the year, and he was a Third Team All-America selection by the Associated Press (AP). Perhaps more important, though, he was an academic All-American too, recording a 3.5 (on a scale of 4.0) grade point average to show the kids who'd taunted him back in high school just how wrong they were.

The spectacular freshman season left Abdur-Rahim with an important decision, one that he would ultimately make and then remake twice. He called one teary press conference to declare that he was turning pro, only to suddenly reverse his decision three weeks later. But in the end, he decided it was best to declare himself eligible for the 1996 NBA draft. Insiders were telling him that he would be one of the first players chosen. And although he was enjoying himself at Cal, the time seemed right to move up, the opportunity too great to pass. "I don't second-guess myself," Abdur-Rahim says now, when asked whether he regrets the decision to leave college less than 13 months after his high school prom. "But sometimes I wish that things might have been a little bit slower because I was having such a good time at Cal."

It was difficult to take things slowly, however, when he knew he could go as high as No. 2 overall in the draft. That had been a dream he had hoped would materialize toward the end of his college career. In fact, until he reached college and dominated in the NCAA, he wasn't sure he'd make the NBA. Suddenly, the goal was attainable right now.

Indeed, it didn't seem like anybody, except perhaps diehard Cal fans, thought declaring for the draft was a bad idea for Abdur-Rahim. If any college freshman was ready for the NBA, it was the slender 6-foot-9 forward with the quick feet, soft touch and solid work ethic. "To me, he's a bigger Scottie Pippen," said NBA draft expert Don Leventhal, who had rated Abdur-Rahim ahead of eventual No. 1 selection Allen Iverson.

Vancouver Grizzlies director of player personnel Larry Riley vividly remembers seeing Abdur-Rahim as a Cal freshman. "What impressed me was the absolute confidence with which he played and the quickness he had around the basket," Riley says now. "He also showed some ability to shoot from the perimeter and he rebounded the ball. But the biggest thing with Shareef is that he always played hard." Riley wasn't the only member of the Grizzlies brass who was instantly impressed. In fact, president and general manager Stu Jackson had long been an Abdur-Rahim admirer, ever since he had seen the 16-year-old Wheeler star three years earlier, during a U.S. Olympic Festival tournament in Colorado Springs in 1993. It didn't take long for the Grizzlies' staff to determine that they wanted Abdur-Rahim. Now they would have to wait to see whether they could land him with the No. 3 pick in the June 26 draft at East Rutherford, New Jersey.

When draft day arrived, the Philadelphia 76ers surprised nobody by selecting Georgetown's electrifying Allen Iverson at No. 1. When the Toronto Raptors announced University of Massachusetts centre Marcus Camby as the No. 2 pick, it was all settled. The Grizzlies would get their man. Back in General Motors Place at Vancouver, British Columbia, where the team was holding a draft party for 9,000 fans, a massive cheer broke out across the arena when Shareef's name was announced by NBA commissioner David Stern. The feeling, it seemed, was mutual. "I can't say I planned this situation," Abdur-Rahim told reporters on draft day. "But I'm happy to be here. I feel like God planned this for me ... I feel like I have an opportunity to be part of something special because the Grizzlies are looking to build, and I feel like I can be a part of that."

Shareef's contract, under the NBA's rookie salary cap at the time, was for three years and would total $7.54 million U.S. The money was the realization of a dream of longterm financial security for both Shareef and his family. His father had recently been the victim of corporate downsizing and was unloading freight on the night shift for an Atlanta trucking company. Shareef didn't want his father to come home with a sore back any more. "It was for my family," he told reporters of his decision to enter the draft. "It was time to give back to them." With an advance on his first contract, he quickly bought his mother a Mercedes and his father a Chevy Suburban. His new-found wealth allowed his father to quit his job and concentrate fulltime on his Muslim ministry. Basketball had indeed proven to be a blessing for the entire Abdur-Rahim family.

Shareef Abdur-Rahim arrived in Vancouver that fall, a 19-year-old in a new city and, to some extent, a new culture. During his first media day with the Grizzlies, when he and other players were required to sit at tables and answer question after question from the local media, Shareef appeared shell-shocked. He came across as so shy and quiet that many reporters were openly wondering whether he was the right player to help sell the game in such a pro-hoops hinterland. Their fears were misplaced. Once Abdur-Rahim got on the court, nobody worried about his quiet nature. They were too busy concentrating on his lightning spin move, his assortment of tasty dunks and his feathery jump hook. Even early on in his rookie season, it was apparent to Grizzlies fans that their new draft pick possessed a special gift. "He may," said Stu Jackson, "have the most upside of anybody in the draft."

When basketball people speak of "upside" they are referring to future potential. Jackson and his scouts obviously had pegged Abdur-Rahim correctly, because he started strongly with the Grizzlies and has improved ever since. In his rookie season, he averaged an impressive 18.7 points per game, but it was evident he was learning every night. From the NBA's All-Star Game onwards, he would average 21.5 points per game and he reached double figures in 59 of his final 61 contests. To conclude his rookie season in style, Abdur-Rahim recorded his first NBA triple-double — 26 points, 10 rebounds and 10 assists — as the Grizzlies downed the Phoenix Suns. He finished third in the NBA's Rookie of the Year balloting and was named to the league's All-Rookie First Team.

Abdur-Rahim's numbers have steadily increased during his first three seasons in the league. But they have been one of few brights spots for the Grizzlies franchise, which has struggled mightily to make any progress in the standings. The team won only 14 of its 82 games during Shareef's rookie season, marking the first time in his basketball career that he had to come to grips with losing almost every night out. They improved to 19 wins the next year and won only eight games in the lockout-shortened, 50-game season of 1998–99.

Nevertheless, Abdur-Rahim's personal numbers have read like a steadily climbing thermometer. In his second NBA season, he averaged 22.3 points, sixth-best in the league and second only to Boston's Antoine Walker among small forwards. In his third season, he bumped that figure up to 23 points per game, fourth best in the league, including a career-high 39-point effort against Boston. His average of 40.4 minutes per contest was fifth highest in the NBA while his .841 percentage from the free-throw line was 18th. If you examine his personal stats since he entered the league, Abdur-Rahim has improved each season in scoring, rebounding, steals, blocked shots and assists, despite playing for arguably the weakest team in the league and facing defensive double teams (where two players would guard him) every night. During the three seasons he has been in the league, only four NBA players have scored more points — Karl Malone, Allen Iverson, Mitch Richmond and Michael Jordan.

Even Shareef's defence, which has long been considered his weak suit, has improved dramatically. When he entered the league, one anonymous general manager caustically said that Abdur-Rahim "couldn't guard a door" — a liability that is difficult to hide considering

most teams have a talented scorer playing the small forward position. But since then, Shareef has worked on
his defence and head coach Brian Hill now plays him in
situations Shareef simply couldn't handle as a younger
player. "Defence is the area that Shareef has to work on
the hardest," Hill conceded before Abdur-Rahim's third
season. "But he knows there are things he needs to work
on and he's willing to work at it. And when you have a
guy like that, there's no ceiling on how much he can
accomplish."

Once again, some of this dedication to self-improve-
ment can probably be attributed to Abdur-Rahim's
Muslim way of life. He is now a wealthy young NBA
star, but he remains firmly rooted in the Islamic faith.
He still prays five times daily, he attends mosque Fri-
days whenever it is possible on the road and he strictly
observes Ramadan. During this Islamic holy period of
fasting, practising Muslims such as Shareef must refrain
from taking food or fluids between the break of dawn
and sundown. Ramadan is a month-long period of pur-
ification and spiritual cleansing observed by millions of
Muslims worldwide to commemorate the period of time
when God revealed the Quran to the prophet
Muhammad through the Angel Gabriel. During this
time, Muslims also refrain from loud talking, arguing,
intercourse and smoking during daylight hours.

The ritual of Ramadan puts an interesting twist on
the pro basketball season, which most players find physically taxing enough on its own. For Abdur-Rahim, and
other Muslims in the NBA including Houston Rockets
star Hakeem Olajuwon, Ramadan means getting up
before sunrise to eat and then not eating again until after sunset, just before game time. If a game is scheduled
for an afternoon, a player must go without water. "This
is far more important than basketball," Abdur-Rahim

told the Vancouver *Province,* when his observation of Ramadan during his rookie season was a big story. "This is a time when I'm more at peace with myself and trying to get more in touch with God."

Abdur-Rahim has described Islam as the cornerstone of his life, the essence from which he builds. But he is not the type to broadcast his deep devotion to his faith or to overwhelm anybody with it. Neither, however, does he try to hide it. In fact, when it was suggested to him prior to his third NBA season that being an overt Muslim might alienate potential sponsors, he simply shook his head. "I think it's all about the kind of guy you are," he said. "And if people shy away from me because I am a Muslim, so be it. You know, that's my belief in God. I'm not going to sacrifice that for anything. I'd give up all this (NBA) for that."

This depth to Abdur-Rahim's personality, which seems to go beyond that of many professional athletes, is another reason he appeals to Vancouver's normally hockey-crazed sports fans. When the Vancouver Canucks hockey team traded away Pavel Bure in 1999, many were suggesting that Abdur-Rahim, with his combination of talent, grace and maturity, could become the most popular pro athlete in the province of British Columbia. Prior to his fourth NBA season, he established a charitable foundation in his name to help underprivileged children in Vancouver and his home state of Georgia. Amongst other charitable acts, the foundation donates 100 tickets per Grizzlies game to needy youngsters.

Says Grizzlies General Manager Stu Jackson: "I don't think it's too much to say to the young people of British Columbia that if you're going to emulate someone in the professional sports ranks, Shareef Abdur-Rahim is not a bad guy to pick." Which is why the Grizzlies and their fans were breathing a collective sigh of relief when, prior to his third season, Abdur-Rahim signed a six-year contract extension. "This is a great moment for our franchise," Jackson told a press conference as the deal was signed.

It was perhaps the understatement of the pre-season. Since entering the NBA, the Grizzlies have had difficulty convincing veteran players, who are predominantly Americans, about the merits of playing in Canada. Vancouver has long been seen as the NBA's final outpost, a sort of basketball Siberia. But Abdur-Rahim's signing would change that perception, at least a little. "Players around the league respect Shareef," said Jackson. "They know how good a player he is. And certainly there's going to be some feeling out there that if it's good enough for him, well, it's going to be good enough for others."

As for his reasons for staying in Canada, rather than heading to a basketball-crazy city such as Chicago or Phoenix, or returning home to Atlanta, Abdur-Rahim says he enjoys Vancouver and feels he has a chance to be part of the construction of something special. And in Vancouver, his talents will not go unappreciated, particularly if the franchise can turn the corner. As his father puts it: "Vancouver is the most fertile of ground."

"Honestly, I thought about (going elsewhere)," Shareef admitted after signing the extension. "But I'm comfortable in Vancouver. I'm very happy. I think the people here think a lot of me. So it's like a home away from home ... More than anything, I just feel blessed." Of course, Abdur-Rahim would receive more media attention in a larger U.S. market. And the fact that he plays on the West Coast means Grizzlies highlights often don't even make the sportscasts or newspapers in Eastern time zones. Does that bother him? "No," he says. "I think in a way it keeps me hungry, it keeps me working. And plus I realize that everybody loves a winner. My motivation is trying to help this team win. If we win, then I'll be a household name." In fact, with the sale of the Grizzlies franchise to a Missouri businessman in September 1999, there's a chance that Shareef may be playing elsewhere than Vancouver for the balance of his career.

His contract extension, worth a staggering $71 million U.S. over six years beginning in the fall of 1999, locked Abdur-Rahim and the Grizzlies franchise together. As Shareef's third season dawned, and with rookie point guard Mike Bibby coming aboard, it seemed as though everything was falling into place for the Grizzlies and their small forward to make a major leap forward. That didn't happen, however. Lumbering centre Bryant "Big Country" Reeves, the Grizzlies' first-ever draft pick, reported to training camp woefully out of shape and things just got worse from there. Veteran point guard Lee Mayberry was lost to injury for most of the season, and so was veteran shooting guard Doug West. The young Grizzlies struggled mightily through the 50-game compacted season.

For most of 1998–99, Abdur-Rahim was the good soldier, quietly working without complaint in a clearly frustrating situation, even though that frustration sometimes showed on his face. In fact, as the criticism rained down on Reeves for his poor conditioning, Abdur-Rahim publicly came to the defence of his beleaguered centre. But toward the end of the season, with losses again mounting, the frustration became too much for even the patient Abdur-Rahim. After one particularly demoralizing loss in March, he told reporters that the Grizzlies were playing like "damn high schoolers out there sometimes." And, "We just haven't really made any progress, from year one to year four ..." he told the Vancouver *Sun* after another defeat in April. "Pressure has to be put on everybody to improve this off-season. Maybe that's what it will take to turn things around, if everyone's jobs are in jeopardy."

Those comments created quite a stir in Vancouver, where the Grizzlies have been afforded an extended grace period by both fans and media. Later, Abdur-Rahim would downplay his comments, stressing that he wasn't suggesting there be any changes in management or coaching staff. He still believes in the future of the Grizzlies but he doesn't want to see another backward slide such as the team experienced in 1999. "I'm still confident in the situation here," he said as his third NBA season came to a close. "I think things are going to get better."

Abdur-Rahim will certainly play a huge role in whatever strides the Grizzlies make. Just 10 days after his third NBA season ended, he was back home in Atlanta, doing two-a-day workouts, concentrating on the weaknesses in his game. His ballhandling still needs improvement, so does his defence. He loves to shoot pool and watch movies in his spare time, but those indulgences come well after basketball. "I'm so young," he says, "I just need to continue to work on everything."

How good can Shareef be? Well, as Grizzlies coach Brian Hill says, when you combine natural talent and athleticism with a willingness to work, there is no ceiling. It's a combination that is essential for a player in a slow building situation with a franchise such as the Grizzlies. "I see a young man who understands what accountability is all about," Hill says of his young star. "More young people today are into instant gratification, rather than accountability and working to earn something and being responsible for their actions. He doesn't want anything handed to him and he's willing to work hard for everything."

"Shareef probably trains harder than anybody else on our team in the off-season," adds Larry Riley, one of the men chiefly responsible for drafting Abdur-Rahim. "I still don't know how good he's going to be, because I don't think he's near the top (of his potential) yet." It's safe to assume that Shareef Abdur-Rahim will maximize that potential. In his way of thinking, to do less would be to fail a God who has blessed him. Above all, Abdur-Rahim seems to live and play by this simple tenet, taught to him by his family and reinforced by his faith: "Remember how you came upon all your accomplishments and stay humble."

Shareef has been fortunate to receive good coaching from that first day as a six-year-old when he excitedly carried home the basketball flyer. But without a doubt, his family and Islam are the foundation on which he has built his accomplishments. When the NBA lockout spoiled much of the 1998–99 season and kept NBA players on the sidelines, Shareef used the time to watch some of his younger brother's high school basketball games and to be in Georgia with his family, which includes eight brothers and sisters. He knows that many others like him aren't as fortunate to have such structure and support in their lives. "That really means a lot," he says. "Without that structure, it would be tough to make it.

"I definitely think I worked hard to get where I'm at," Shareef adds. "But there are people out there who worked just as hard as I did and didn't make it. I just think God put me in a situation where he let me accomplish these things. And it's not just the things that have happened in relation to basketball — there are lots of things outside the court, too. I just believe that God blessed me."

REEF BY NUMBERS

Name: Julius Shareef Abdur-Rahim
Nicknames: "Reef," "The Future"
Position: Small forward, Vancouver Grizzlies
Born: December 11, 1976; Atlanta, GA
Height: 6'9"   **Weight**: 230 lbs.
High school: Wheeler, Marietta, GA
College: University of California at Berkeley, Berkeley, CA
Drafted: 1996, No. 3 overall by Vancouver Grizzlies

COLLEGE
As a freshman (1995–96)
28 games; 972 minutes; .518 from field; .381 from three-point range; .683 from free-throw line; 236 total rebounds; 8.4 rebounds per game; 29 total assists; 1.0 assists per game; 590 total points; 21.1 points per game.
College Honours
1995–96 — Associated Press Third Team All-American; Pacific-10 Conference Player of the Year; All-Pac-10 and Pac-10 Freshman of the Year; John Wooden Award finalist.
College Records
First Pac-10 freshman to be named Player of the Year; led freshmen in scoring; set Cal freshman record for points, scoring average, field goals and free-throws in a season.

NBA
1996–97 (Grizzlies)
80 games; 71 games started; 2,802 total minutes; 35 minutes per game; .453 from field; .259 from three-point range; .746 from free-throw line; 555 total rebounds; 6.9 rebounds per game; 175 total assists; 2.2 assists per game; 79 blocks; 79 steals; 1,494 total points; 18.7 points per game.
1997–98 (Grizzlies)
82 games; 82 games started; 2,950 total minutes; 36 minutes per game; .485 from field; .412 from three-point range; .784 from free-throw line; 581 total rebounds; 7.1 rebounds per game; 213 total assists; 2.6 assists per game; 76 blocks; 89 steals; 1,829 total points; 22.3 points per game.

1998–99 (Grizzlies)

50 games; 50 games started; 2,021 total minutes; 40.4 minutes per game; .432 from field; .306 from three-point range; .841 from free-throw line; 374 total rebounds; 7.5 rebounds per game; 172 total assists; 3.4 assists per game; 55 blocks; 69 steals; 1,152 total points; 23.0 points per game.

NBA career to date (1996–99)

212 games; 203 games started; 7,773 total minutes; 36.7 minutes per game; .460 from field; .342 from three-point range; .787 from free-throw line; 1,510 total rebounds; 7.1 rebounds per game; 560 total assists; 2.6 assists per game; 210 blocks; 237 steals; 4,475 total points; 21.1 points per game.

NBA honours

1996–97 — Finished third in NBA Rookie of the Year balloting behind Allen Iverson and Stephon Marbury; selected to NBA All-Rookie First Team.

Sources

Victoria *Times Colonist*

Vancouver *Sun*

Vancouver *Province*

Atlanta *Journal-Constitution*

Canadian Press

Associated Press

Vancouver Grizzlies media guides

Official NBA Register, (regular-season) Guide and Draft Media Guide

NBA.com

KOBE BRYANT

Before he had reached his 18th birthday, he was chosen in the NBA draft. Before he was old enough to vote, he was made a millionaire several times over. Before he left high school, he escorted pop star Brandy to his senior prom. Before he had hoisted his very first shot at his very first NBA training camp, he had already starred in his very own basketball shoe commercial. To say that Kobe Bryant works on a unique timetable is like saying Mozart was a pretty talented young musician.

Just as Kevin Garnett was a special case in 1995, when he jumped straight from high school to the highest level of professional basketball, so was Bryant exactly one year later. Bryant differed from all other prep-to-pro leapers in NBA history in one major regard, however: He wasn't a big man. He was a quick, athletic, six-foot-six guard, the sort of player who seems to be a dime a dozen in the NBA. For the Pennsylvania prepster to attempt the jump was even more daunting a proposition than Garnett's. "I didn't see him as a can't-miss guy," Vancouver Grizzlies director of player personnel Larry Riley admits. "I think (back in 1996) there was some opportunity that he could fail."

He hasn't failed, of course. Far from it. In fact, during his first three professional seasons, Kobe Bryant has evolved into a certified celebrity. Some suggest his star power is much greater than his actual accomplishments on the basketball court. Still, his talent and style are undeniable and his status as an icon for young fans would be difficult for any current player to match. When Michael Jordan announced his retirement prior to the 1998–99 NBA season, the name that cropped up most often as people speculated on the "Air Apparent" was Kobe Bryant. Other young NBAers have put up better numbers and made more of an impact on their team's success during the past three years. But none have shown the creative genius, the mid-air majesty and the full-court charisma of the young man who wears Number 8 for the Los Angeles Lakers. How else do you explain the fact that, at 19 years old, Kobe Bryant was voted by fans to be an NBA All-Star Game starter — long before he was a starter on his own team?

The story of Bryant's rapid rise to the NBA is as interesting as it is unique. There may never be another player like Kobe simply because there may never again be the same set of circumstances that produced Kobe. Bryant is the son of a former NBAer, journeyman forward Joe "Jelly Bean" Bryant, who played eight years in the league for Philadelphia, San Diego and Houston during the mid-1970s through the early 1980s. Kobe, who was named after a Japanese steak dish that his parents saw on a restaurant menu, certainly possessed the proper genes and was exposed to the highest level of the game at an early age. But unlike other children of North American pro athletes, Bryant spent eight formative years of his childhood living and attending school in Europe. Instead of incubating in a hoops hot-spot like Chicago or Philadelphia or New York, young Kobe practised his moves in the basketball isolation of Italy, where the Bryant family, including older sisters Sharia and Shaya, moved in 1984 after Joe's NBA career had run its course.

During the family's time overseas, Kobe learned to speak fluent Italian and was exposed to cultural experiences that would not have been possible in the United States. He also received a rich education in basketball. He would often attend practices with his father's Italian pro teams — something he couldn't have done had Joe been playing in the NBA. And when he wasn't being schooled in the finer points of the game by his father or his father's teammates, Kobe pored over the videotapes of Lakers games regularly sent overseas by relatives and his father's scouting services. While watching those tapes, he would study the best moves of his favourite players and then strive to imitate them. In particular, he admired the play of Lakers-great Magic Johnson. He absorbed as much as he could from the tapes, then grabbed a ball and incorporated those moves into his game through hour upon hour of work. "I was like a computer," Bryant told *Sports Illustrated* in 1998. "I retrieved information to benefit my game."

Italian friends warned him he would be just another player when the family eventually returned to the U.S. But they were wrong. In 1991, the Bryants moved back to Philadelphia, where Joe had gone to the NBA finals with the 76ers the year before Kobe was born. During the next few years, Kobe not only developed into a star, he became the best high school player in the entire country. Over his four years as a starter at suburban Lower Merion High School, Bryant piled up 2,883 points, breaking the legendary Wilt Chamberlain's southeastern Pennsylvania scoring record (2,359) as well as that of successor Carlin Warley (2,441). Lower Merion won 77 games and lost just 13 during Bryant's final three seasons with the team.

As a junior, Bryant averaged 31 points, 10 rebounds, five blocks, four assists and four steals a game. He was named Pennsylvania state Player of the Year by both *USA Today* and the Philadelphia *Inquirer*, although his team was knocked out of the state playoffs. During Bryant's senior year at the school (1995–96), he posted averages of 30.8 points, 12 rebounds, 6.5 assists, 3.8 blocks and four steals to power Lower Merion to the Class AAA state championship and a sterling 31–3 overall record. In one game against Marple Newtown, Bryant poured in 50 points. In another virtuoso performance in the District 1 Class AAA title game against Chester, he scored 34 points and added 15 rebounds, six assists and nine blocks.

The list of high school honours coming his way after that standout senior season was lengthy. Bryant was named National Prep Player of the Year by both *USA Today* and *Parade Magazine*. He was also the Naismith and Gatorade Circle of Champions Player of the Year and he was selected to the McDonald's All-America team. Bryant was also a strong student, making the Lower Merion honour role and posting an SAT score of 1,080. Academically he would have been eligible to enter most schools in the country, and he liked the idea of attending Duke, North Carolina or Michigan. But there was one place that sounded more appealing than any college — the NBA. "I know I'll have to work extra hard and I know it's a big step," Bryant told reporters after making his decision. "I can do it."

In 1975, Kobe's father Joe had gone to the NBA, leaving La Salle University after his junior season for the lure of the pro dollars. But the money available to Kobe in 1996 was much greater than when his father had been drafted. Joe Bryant had been paid a reported total of $900,000 U.S. over five years on his first NBA contract. His son would almost certainly make more than that in just one season. In 1995, Kevin Garnett had broken the barrier for prep players in the current era by becoming the first high-schooler since 1975 to make the leap directly to the NBA. By the time Bryant announced his decision, Garnett had posted a successful rookie season in Minnesota, so the precedent had been firmly established. But Kobe Bryant was drawing interest, and also considerable skepticism, for trying to make the move as a smaller skill player.

Among the skeptics was Charlotte Hornets owner George Shinn. Ironically, Shinn's team drafted Kobe Bryant, calling the youngster's name 13th overall on June 26 in Continental Airlines Arena. The Hornets were simply selecting the high schooler for the Los Angeles Lakers, however. The teams then subsequently arranged a trade that saw Los Angeles send veteran centre Vlade Divac to Charlotte in exchange for Kobe Bryant. When the deal was finalized, a delighted Shinn described it as the greatest trade in the history of basketball.

Lakers vice-president Jerry West was obviously thrilled as well, and willing to take a gamble on Bryant. West had been bowled over by the high school hotshot's private workout with the Lakers prior to the draft. In fact, West would later describe Bryant as the best young player he had ever worked out.

The trade paid off for the Lakers in more than one way. Not only were they able to land Bryant, whom West felt had the potential to be a great player, but by trading Divac they were able to clear enough salary cap money to sign free-agent prize Shaquille O'Neal. As well, Kobe Bryant brought a distinct star quality to L.A., a town with an appetite for such things. In fact, fans didn't wait until the season started to check out the rookie en masse. When Bryant suited up for his first FILA summer league game with the Lakers in July at Long Beach State, the building was sold out.

"Everybody had come to see Kobe," recalls Ken Shields, the former Canadian national team coach, who was in the stands for that game. "In the first five minutes, Kobe did a couple of things that just blew me away. I think he had 17 free throws in the game. No one could guard him. No one could stay with him. He just oozed so much potential." Indeed, this was a teenager who had yet to fill out physically, but who already had an arsenal of eye-popping offensive moves that were Jordanesque. Bryant was so quick, so fluid, so well-balanced, so confident. He seemed to be able to hang in the air longer than his defenders. And when he exploded to the hoop, he had more than enough hops to finish with a creative dunk.

One on one, there would be few players who could shut down Bryant, even as a rookie. But the NBA is about a lot more than one-on-one skills and Bryant knew there would be players lining up to deliver him lessons. He relished the challenge. "That's one of the reasons I wanted to come to the NBA — because I knew opponents were going to come at me, talk a little trash," he later told *NBA Inside Stuff* magazine. "I knew I'd come into the game and (the opposing) coach would run an isolation play and try to post me up. I wanted that challenge. I wanted to show them that, hey, I'm a basketball player and I'm going to come right back at you."

As a rookie, without the benefit of any college tutelage, Bryant had much to learn, however. He had to learn the difference between good and bad shots; he had to learn how to play NBA defence; and he had to learn the intricacies of the team game at the pro level. Much of that learning would come in practice and on the bench. On November 3, 1996, Bryant became the youngest player to ever appear in an NBA game, at 18 years, two months and 11 days. But for his entire rookie season, he would average only 15.5 minutes per game and score at a 7.6-point-per-game clip while playing a combination of backup shooting guard, point guard and small forward for veteran head coach Del Harris. And when Bryant complained mildly about a lack of minutes early during that first season, Harris made his position clear. "He's elected to come into a man's game at the age of 18," the Lakers coach told the Salt Lake *Tribune*. "He's got to play and live in a man's world. You can't be unfair to other players just because he is 18. He's got to earn his own way."

Bryant has since said that he was sometimes frustrated during that rookie season with the lack of playing time because it didn't allow him to show opponents — and skeptics — that he was capable of playing the NBA game. But he has also admitted that he learned a lot on the bench watching veterans such as the Lakers' Eddie Jones, then the team's starter. "When I made the decision to go into the NBA from high school, I was 110 percent sure I could compete with these guys," Bryant told the Vancouver *Province* during that rookie season. "I realize now it's irrelevant how much time I get to play right now. I have to work on my game every day in practice and when I do get to play, the focus has to be on what's right for the team. I've got a lot of work to do to develop into the right kind of player I want to be."

Despite his relatively minor minutes with the Lakers, Bryant managed to score in double figures 25 times as a rookie, including one late-season roll in which he accomplished this feat seven times in 10 games. He was also able to make a dramatic impact on the NBA during All-Star Weekend in Cleveland. He shone in the Rookie All-Star Game, scoring a record 31 points and adding eight rebounds. Then he won the league's slam dunk competition. "I wanted to come out and show everyone that even though I wasn't playing much, don't forget about me," Bryant would later tell *NBA Inside Stuff.*

Everyone would remember Bryant's performance at Cleveland. Unfortunately, the way he concluded his rookie campaign would also be burned into most fans' minds. The Lakers faced Utah in the second round of the 1997 playoffs and, in the decisive Game 5 with the score deadlocked at 89 and the Lakers holding the final possession, Del Harris diagramed the play for Bryant. Guarded closely by Bryon Russell, the rookie fired up an air ball at the regulation buzzer. Kobe would shoot three more air balls in overtime as the Lakers lost 98–93 and were eliminated from the post-season. "Tonight I just didn't come through," Bryant told *USA Today* after perhaps the toughest learning experience of his rookie year. "But play the game again, and I want the ball again." The next morning, bright and early, Bryant was back in the gym at UCLA, working toward his second NBA season.

The work would definitely pay off. In Year 2, Bryant became the Lakers' sixth man, a sort of super-sub for coach Del Harris. His minutes on the court rose substantially and his point production more than doubled to 15.4 per game, the best of any non-starter in the NBA. At a time when most players his age were worrying about sophomore exams, he had already become a consistent scorer off the bench for the Lakers, hitting double figures in 65 of his 79 regular-season games. "I don't think anyone has any questions about his God-given talent as a basketball player," Billy Cunningham told *NBA Inside Stuff* in January of 1998. "It's going to take a little time, but if he refines his defensive skills, Kobe Bryant is earmarked for greatness."

At times during Bryant's second season, that potential for greatness was on full display. In a December

17 matchup in Chicago against the league-champion Chicago Bulls and Michael Jordan, Bryant scored 33 points in 29 minutes. During one stretch of just under 13 minutes against Houston five days earlier, he poured in 27 points. But the biggest breakthrough of that 1997–98 season came with his selection to the NBA All-Star Game in New York. In league-wide fan balloting, Bryant was named a starter for the Western Conference squad despite the fact he didn't even start for the Lakers. "Kobe's going to be an All-Star for many years to come," Del Harris told the New York *Daily News*. "His being voted a starter kind of messed up on my system of bringing him along slowly, but I can deal with that."

At 19 years and five months, Bryant became the youngest all-star in NBA history, beating his idol Magic Johnson, who played in the 1980 classic at 20 years, five months. The hype machine, meanwhile, was in full effect. The NBA and the media painted the 1998 All-Star Game as a kind of colossal one-on-one matchup between the East's Michael Jordan and his successor, the West's Kobe Bryant. "It's a little weird," Bryant admitted to reporters covering the game in New York. "Two years ago, I was winning a state championship in high school. Now here I am in the All-Star Game. I know I'm going to be nervous."

Nervous is certainly not something Bryant appeared to be as the game unfolded. He scored 18 points, including one flashy behind-the-back dribble for a dunk, in his all-star debut to lead the Western Conference squad offensively. But he hoisted 16 shots in just 22 minutes to get those points. His decision to shoot so often with so many other talented players on the floor may have thrown some noses out of joint. When he waved off a screen set by Western teammate Karl Malone, he angered the Utah veteran. For whatever reasons, coach

George Karl kept Bryant on the bench for the fourth quarter of the game.

Bryant's All-Star status didn't carry much weight with his own coach in Los Angeles, either. It didn't stop Del Harris from curbing his second-year player's minutes when his performance began to tail off midway through the season. "He didn't learn (the team game) in high school and he didn't go to college, so he has to learn it here," Harris told *Sports Illustrated*. "The only way he can learn it is by reduced playing time until he accepts it."

During Bryant's second trip to the post-season, Harris limited his minutes to 20 per game, down six minutes per contest from what he had played during the regular season. The sophomore pro averaged 8.7 points off the bench as the Lakers advanced to the conference finals before being swept by the Jazz. Despite the uneven nature of his first two seasons, the Lakers were willing to make a major financial commitment to their young star. In January of 1999, just after the NBA lockout had been lifted, the team signed Bryant to a six-year contract extension that will run through the 2004–5 season and guarantee him $71 million U.S., the maximum allowed under the collective bargaining agreement. The final year of the deal will pay Bryant $14.62 million. He will be only 26 years old when it expires.

Some of the funds will go back to the community through the Kobe Bryant Foundation, a charitable organization started in 1998 and dedicated to helping at-risk youth in southern California. "I've loved my two years with the Lakers and am looking forward to the future," he told reporters on the day the deal was signed. "The team, the fans and the city have been so supportive and great to me. I'm thrilled with my new contract extension and hope and plan to be a Laker for life."

"We're very pleased to get this contract done," added Lakers vice-president Jerry West. "As I've said since we traded for Kobe back in 1996, we think he's one of the most talented young players in the NBA. He's going to continue to improve and make us a better team as he does so, and we're glad to know that he'll be a Laker for years to come."

Bryant's improvement was most obvious during his third season in the NBA. In the lockout-shortened 1998–99 campaign, he became a starter for the Lakers, first at small forward and, after Eddie Jones was traded to Charlotte, at his more natural position of shooting guard. While starting all 50 games of the regular season, his numbers rose dramatically. Bryant averaged 37.9 minutes, 19.9 points, 5.3 rebounds and 3.8 assists. He also shot at a highly respectable .465 clip from the field and .839 from the free-throw line. Bryant led the Lakers in steals, with 1.44 per game, and finished among the NBA's top 20 in scoring (15th) and free-throw percentage (20th). He also made the All-NBA Third Team.

It was a season in which Bryant turned in some eye-opening performances. Against the Denver Nuggets, he had 26 points and career highs of 13 rebounds and nine assists. But perhaps the finest moment was his career-high 38-point effort in a nationally televised game in Orlando, when he scored 33 points in the second half alone to dig the Lakers out of a 20-point hole. That performance prompted Los Angeles *Times* beat writer Tim Kawakami to wonder if Bryant wasn't the team's young Elvis. "He's raw," wrote Kawakami, "but no matter who's on stage with him, he's pretty much the show."

Nevertheless, there remain some criticisms of Bryant's game. It has been characterized as too erratic, too undisciplined and too individualistic to make him a true superstar in the NBA. When making those criticisms, however, it seems people are forgetting his age. In 1999, as he began his fourth season in the NBA, most other players his age were just beginning their senior years in college. Bryant is already a veteran and he has nearly his entire career still ahead of him. The word "potential" is still very much legitimate when discussing Kobe Bryant.

Coach Del Harris, who was fired during the 1999 season as the talented Lakers struggled, sometimes cited Bryant's lack of understanding of team basketball. His teammates have also been critical of Bryant's liberal shot selection. And during that season, one storyline that cropped up was whether or not Kobe and Shaq could ever co-exist on a championship team. "It did catch me off guard a little bit, people scrutinizing my game," Bryant admitted to the Los Angeles *Times* during the 1999 playoffs. "That's good, I guess. That means they care about you. Some of the mistakes I made were pretty much honest mistakes. It wasn't like mistakes only I make. I think more than anything, they're more magnified because of my potential, because of my talent. People want me to learn quickly, which I'm trying to do."

Bryant's success, both on and off the court, has far outweighed negatives that have come from jumping directly to the NBA. And his progress and profile are serving to push other talented high schoolers toward a similar leap. In the 1996 draft, Jermaine O'Neal went 17th overall to the Portland Trail Blazers. In 1997, Tracy McGrady was selected ninth overall out of Durham, North Carolina, by the Toronto Raptors. Al Harrington, out of Elizabeth, New Jersey, went 25th to Indiana in 1998. And in 1999, Jonathan Bender of Picayune, Mississippi, was taken fifth by the Raptors before Chicago's Leon Smith went 29th to the Dallas Mavericks.

Of all these players, however, none were as NBA-ready as either Kevin Garnett or Kobe Bryant. And while scouts across the league must now somewhat reluctantly evaluate high schoolers for every draft, most will tell you that the prep player who is truly ready for pro basketball is a very rare one indeed.

Much to the chagrin of many scouts, only two of the 11 high schoolers who have declared for the draft since 1995 have gone unchosen, and the seven selected before 1999 are all still in the league. But the experience of Rashard Lewis, the Texas prep phenomenon who was in tears during the 1998 draft as he was passed over during the entire first round, has probably made high schoolers think twice about making the decision. Still, Lewis eventually went 32nd overall to the Seattle SuperSonics and started seven games for Seattle during the lockout-shortened 1998–99 season. "Kobe and Kevin Garnett make the game look easy for high school players to come out," Lewis told NBA.com in a 1999 feature on the subject. "But it's not easy. It's a job out there."

Many people have emphasized that Kobe Bryant, much like Kevin Garnett, possessed an unusual level of maturity for a high schooler, something that helped him to make a relatively smooth transition to the NBA. And as a young rookie, Bryant was also able to enjoy stability at home because his entire family moved from Philadelphia to Los Angeles along with him in 1996. In fact, as a young NBA "veteran", Bryant still lived with his parents.

Bryant was also fortunate to make the leap from high school to a solid NBA franchise. The Lakers were no struggling expansion team — they've won 11 league championships. Bryant has appreciated the solidity of the team and the support of its fans. "I was lucky. I came to a team that had Shaq, Eddie (Jones) — who I knew from back home in Philadelphia — Byron Scott and Jerome (Kersey)," he told *NBA Inside Stuff* magazine. "I had a lot of experienced people around who could help me."

Kobe Bryant also had some valuable childhood experiences upon which to draw. Growing up in Europe, he says, helped him to cope with all the down time an NBA player spends on the road, often by himself. "I'd rather not go out," he told the Los Angeles *Times* during the 1999 season. "I stay in my hotel room ... I've always been by myself. Remember, I was raised overseas. It was always just me, by myself. Just me and the game." Of course, the fact that his father was a professional basketball player didn't hurt, although Bryant has said his dad being a pro wasn't a huge factor in his basketball development. "My father was just good at being my dad," he says. "He encouraged me to play a lot of sports ... But my father wasn't there to really push me towards a certain direction. He was just there as a father. I think just being around my father, period — that helped me more than anything. Because people would come up to me and say my dad is a great basketball player. But he's even a better person."

Kobe Bryant was once asked by *NBA Inside Stuff* if he ever regretted jumping to the league straight from high school. "No, not at all," he said. "The competitiveness — playing against the best basketball players in the world, guarding Scottie Pippen, Penny Hardaway, Michael Jordan — it's all been fun."

KID KOBE

Name: Kobe B. Bryant
Position: Guard/Forward
Born: August 23, 1978; Philadelphia, PA
Height: 6'7" **Weight:** 210 lbs.
High school: Lower Merion, Philadelphia, PA
College: None
Drafted: 1996, No. 13 overall, by Charlotte Hornets; rights traded to Los Angeles Lakers on July 11, 1996

NBA
1996–97 (Lakers)
71 games; 6 games started; 1,103 total minutes; 15.5 minutes per game; .417 from field; .375 from three-point range; .819 from free-throw line; 132 total rebounds; 1.9 rebounds per game; 91 total assists; 1.3 assists per game; 23 blocks; 49 steals; 539 total points; 7.6 points per game.
1997–98 (Lakers)
79 games; 1 game started; 2,056 total minutes; 26.0 minutes per game; .428 from field; .341 from three-point range; .794 from free-throw line; 242 total rebounds; 3.1 rebounds per game; 199 total assists; 2.5 assists per game; 40 blocks; 74 steals; 1,220 total points; 15.4 points per game.
1998–99 (Lakers)
50 games; 50 games started; 1,896 total minutes; 37.9 minutes per game; .465 from field; .267 from three-point range; .839 from free-throw line; 264 total rebounds; 5.3 rebounds per game; 190 total assists; 3.8 assists per game; 50 blocks; 72 steals; 996 total points; 19.9 points per game.
Career to date (1996–99)
200 games; 57 games started; 5,055 total minutes; 25.3 minutes per game; .439 from field; .335 from three-point range; .813 from free-throw line; 638 total rebounds; 3.2 rebounds per game; 480 total assists; 2.4 assists per game; 113 blocks; 195 steals; 2,755 total points; 13.8 points per game.
Playoffs to date (1997, '98 and '99)
28 games; 8 games started; 668 total minutes; 23.9 minutes per game; .414 from field; .283 from three-point range; .773 from free-throw line; 87 total rebounds; 3.1 rebounds per game;

64 total assists; 2.3 assists per game; 20 blocks; 21 steals; 328 total points; 11.7 points per game.

NBA honours

1996–97 — NBA All-Rookie Second Team; Nestle Crunch Slam Dunk championship winner

1997–98 — Voted as a starter for Western Conference in 1998 NBA All-Star Game

1998–99 — All-NBA Third Team

Sources

Sports Illustrated feature, April 27, 1998

NBA Inside Stuff interview, January, 1998

Los Angeles *Times*

Dallas *Morning News*

Vancouver *Province*

USA Today

Associated Press

Canadian Press

Official NBA Register, (regular-season) Guide and Draft Media Guide

NBA.com

New York *Daily News*

Salt Lake *Tribune*

VINCE CARTER

It was Vince Carter's greatest individual moment in professional basketball to date. The high-flying swingman had just been named NBA Rookie of the Year. And there flanking the handsome young Toronto Raptors star were his beaming parents.

This was no mere photo opportunity, however — no case of parents basking in their child's reflected glory. This is just the way it is, the way it has always been. Vince Carter's family is extremely supportive. And if you were looking for the biggest reason why Carter was accepting the Eddie Gottlieb Trophy for Rookie of the Year in May of 1999, you wouldn't have to look any further than the proud couple standing beside him.

"A large part of Vince's success is that he was just blessed with an incredible physical talent, a physical gift," says Carter's high school coach, Charles Brinkerhoff. "But an equal part is his work ethic. And just as important, I would say, is his character, which comes from his home life."

Vince Carter's home life was perhaps atypical when compared to that of many NBA players. He and his younger brother, Christopher, were raised in the comfortable, middle-class, Daytona Beach, Florida, home of two career educators. His mother, Michelle Carter-Robinson, was a teacher for 20 years, the last five of which were spent as an elementary and middle school discipline specialist before she retired in 1998. "If you got in trouble," she laughs, "you saw me." Vince's stepfather, Harry Robinson, spent 36 years as an educator and was the band director at his sons' high school before retiring in 1997. Both parents have their master's degrees and both stressed the importance of education in their sons' lives. And both were constantly there for Vince as he blossomed into one of the finest young basketball players on the planet and — those who deal with him regularly will attest — a personable young man.

Indeed, there is little doubt about his parents' positive influence on Vince Carter's life. When NBA observers laud his humility, his generous smile and his easygoing personality almost as much as his hair-raising, high-wire act around the hoop, Carter is quick to credit his family as his foundation. They have been there through everything — through the years of minor football when the tall, wiry quarterback eluded tacklers, to the soccer fields and the volleyball courts of his youth. Vince was always interested in sports and his parents were always interested in what he was doing.

They were also interested in homework. Their rule was simple: Vince came home from school, had a snack and went straight to the books. Then, if there was time, he could pursue the games he loved. As a result, Vince's grades were good. So was his game. He began competitive basketball when he was seven, typically playing a couple of years above his age group because he was taller, and his skill level higher, than most boys his age. By the time he hit seventh grade, he stood five-foot-eight and could already dunk. "He was always the go-to little boy," his mother says now.

Not much changed when Vince entered Daytona Beach Mainland High. The skinny, six-foot-one ninth-grader managed to make the varsity team and start at point guard, averaging about 12 points a game for the Buccaneers, who finished 15–16 that season. In his sophomore year, Carter's stats rose dramatically as he averaged 19.9 points and six rebounds per game to help lead Mainland to a 21–6 record and a spot in the districts, the first level of Florida state playoffs. His high school star shot through the roof as a junior, when he pumped in 28 points per game, hauled down 11 rebounds and averaged nearly five assists to lead the Buccaneers to a 32–2 record and a berth in the state semifinals.

"He was a slasher, an intimidator, with some huge dunks in high school," recalls coach Charles Brinkerhoff. "The things people are watching now (in the NBA), Vince was doing those things in high school — sometimes even more," Brinkerhoff adds, "because there was less pressure here on him if something didn't work."

Brinkerhoff remembers Carter as "fierce, competitive and intense" with tremendous athletic ability. Yet he was also unselfish, particularly for a player of his calibre. "A lot of Vince's character is to be a team player, which is unusual for a guy of his ability," Brinkerhoff says. "You knew all along he had the ability to do these things. But he was reluctant to take *all* the shots."

Interestingly, Vince Carter's scoring average would actually drop from his junior to his senior year in high school. He would score at a 25.6-point clip in his final prep season, but his rebounds climbed to 12 per game and his assists to 6.5. Most important, with Carter leading the way, the Buccaneers captured the Florida state 6A championship with a 34–2 record, beating perennial national power Miami High in the semifinals and Fort Lauderdale Dillard in the title game. At the end of the season, Mainland was ranked 15th in the nation by *USA Today*.

But Vince was no one-dimensional hoopster during high school. He had taken music lessons since the fifth grade and played the alto, tenor and baritone saxophone. Besides being the basketball star in his senior year, he was also the drum major for his stepfather's Mainland marching band, earning a scholarship offer for music to Bethune-Cookman. He wrote poetry and even helped pen the Mainland homecoming song. He was also an All-County volleyball player until he had to quit the sport in his senior year because his time commitment to basketball and band was simply too heavy.

Mostly, though, Vince Carter had become known across the state for his incredible basketball prowess. During his junior and senior seasons at Mainland, there was never much room in the school's 800-capacity gym. In fact, people sometimes paid five dollars apiece to watch games via closed-circuit TV on campus. For one matchup against crosstown rival Seabreeze during Carter's senior year, the Buccaneers attracted a crowd of 6,400 to the Daytona Beach Ocean Center.

By the time he left high school, Carter had grown from a six-foot-one, 155-pound freshman to a six-foot-six, 190-pound senior who was providing Florida prep fans with plenty of thrills. Highlight video of his high school dunks made it seem as if he were playing on eight-foot baskets. "I can't think of any greater Florida high school player," says Brinkerhoff, who coached Mainland to two more state titles since Carter graduated. "There have been no other (NBA) rookies of the year out of Florida."

Carter had become one of the most sought-after college recruits in the nation. Seventy-seven schools, including every top program in the U.S., had been courting him since before his junior season, when he began attending some of the country's major all-star summer basketball camps. It was a potentially confusing time for a young man. But once again, Carter's parents were there to help him through. They quickly narrowed the list of suitors down to a workable number. "Seventy-seven schools are *not* coming here on home visits," his mother said. The list was weeded to nine, then to six: Kansas, Kentucky, Duke, Florida, Florida State and North Carolina were all permitted to visit.

Michelle and Harry approached the task of choosing Vince's school in a highly organized manner. They made a chart listing each university and several categories, including academic standards, dormitories, school location, the atmosphere of the basketball program and even whether the coaches' families were involved with the team. Schools received check marks depending on how they fared in each category.

The University of North Carolina, a Chapel Hill campus with an illustrious history in college basketball, ultimately received the most check marks, and Vince and his parents were able to survive the recruiting process with their sanity intact. Time management and organization had been essential. Vince also had to keep up with his grade 12 schoolwork and the plethora of all-star games and awards functions to which he was invited. "I'm proud of the way we handled it," Michelle Carter-Robinson says now.

Despite the fact he had battled the rest of the country to land Carter's services, North Carolina head coach Dean Smith didn't seem intent on over-using the freshman, who didn't play the type of defense demanded by the Tar Heels (as the North Carolina team was called). Carter would average less than 18 minutes per game during his first college season, getting less than six shots per contest as he struggled to find his place in the Carolina system. He would finish the season averaging 7.5

points and 3.8 rebounds, surrounded by loud whispers that he wasn't living up to his high school hype and was ill-equipped to play Atlantic Coast Conference (ACC) defence.

Back home, Mom wasn't buying it. Her son had been an outstanding prep defender at Mainland. "It was very upsetting to hear at first, that he can't play defence, this and that," Michelle Carter-Robinson recalls. "I just thought to myself: 'What had he been doing down here?' I quickly realized there were a lot of politics involved in sports at that level."

Carter's high school coach believes that Vince's early struggles at Carolina were somewhat overblown by the media. It was only natural that a high school star would have to adjust his game in such a celebrated college basketball mecca. Brinkerhoff does concede, however, that Carter needed improvement on his footwork and ballhandling. He had often relied on his athletic ability in high school, where he could simply elevate above the competition and decide what to do from there. In the ACC, he would have to become a more complete player.

It has been said that Vince Carter was an outstanding athlete coming out of high school and that the North Carolina experience made him an outstanding basketball player. That is probably an oversimplification. But there is also an element of truth to it. "Comparing high school ball to North Carolina is like comparing grammar school to Harvard," Brinkerhoff says. "With (coaches) Dean Smith and Bill Guthridge, he learned so much at North Carolina. I have no problem with that statement ... there has got to be natural development when an athlete is working with a fabulous coach (like Smith or Guthridge). But at Mainland he was *not* just an athlete who ran up and down the court."

Carter himself has described how North Carolina

coaches "break down your game" at Chapel Hill. "You relearn the game," he told Fox Sports' *The Last Word.* "It (the North Carolina experience) helped me most probably with the coaching staff, taking my game from scratch, breaking it down and teaching us all how the game should be played," Carter added. "That has helped a lot of players become NBA players."

This process also led to some early frustration in college, but Carter could take some comfort in the fact that he was part of a program that had produced a litany of talented NBA players. And the struggling freshman even received a little helpful advice from the school's most famous alumnus, Michael Jordan, who spoke with Carter in the summer before his sophomore year. "I really don't recall the circumstances," Carter would later tell the Toronto *Sun,* "only that Michael told me my time will come."

It certainly did. And soon. As a sophomore, Vince improved his defense and nearly doubled his minutes on the floor, bumping up his scoring average to 13 points per game, third best on the Tar Heels, while also chipping in 4.5 rebounds and 2.4 assists per night. He finished 13th among ACC scorers and made third team all-conference. As Carolina moved through the National Collegiate Athletic Association (NCAA) Tournament, he was named to the All-East Regional team and he finished the season with 21 points, six rebounds and four steals in a national semifinal loss to eventual champion Arizona. Meanwhile, Vince Carter was quickly becoming known across the country for his highlight-reel dunks.

In his junior — and, as it would turn out, his final — year at North Carolina, Carter raised his rebounding and scoring numbers yet again, finishing with 15.6 points and 5.1 rebounds per game. He led the Atlantic

Coast Conference in field goal percentage at .591, a figure which ranked him 18th nationally. During his final NCAA Tournament, he averaged 18.2 points and shot a team high .590 from the field including a season-high 24 points in a victory over UNC-Charlotte.

By the time his junior season was over, Carter had been named a first-team All-ACC pick and a second-team All-American and he had fulfilled the promise of his prep press clippings. He had also been left with a decision: Did he leave college for the NBA draft or stay in school for his senior year?

Once again, Carter's parents were there to help. Michelle and Harry flew to Chapel Hill to meet with Dean Smith and Bill Guthridge. The Carolina coaches told Vince's parents where they thought their son would be drafted. Vince and his parents returned to their hotel room and discussed it. Then Vince made the choice. He would enter the draft.

"I don't think it was overly tough," Michelle Carter-Robinson says now. "We weighed all the pros and cons. Basketball-wise, we felt he was ready."

Others felt the same way. "Vince is a very good athlete, probably the best at running and jumping of any player in the draft," offered Vancouver Grizzlies director of player personnel Larry Riley. "He's a very flashy player and if there were a dunk contest he would win it. The question on him is he played in a system at North Carolina where he didn't play the one-on-one game, so can he develop the types of one-on-one moves that are necessary in the NBA? I think he will. I think he will be a high-level performer in the NBA."

So did the Toronto Raptors. Although they didn't actually draft Carter in June of 1998, they did plan to obtain him all along. On draft day, the Raptors selected Carter's Carolina teammate and good friend Antawn

Jamison at No. 4, knowing that Golden State was interested in Jamison. The Warriors then took Carter at No. 5 before immediately shipping him and some cash to Toronto for Jamison. The two Tar Heel teammates simply exchanged NBA team hats, and smiles, following this draft day swap.

The Raptors had done their homework. They had been impressed by Vince's athleticism in his pre-draft workout, when he shook off the effects of an injury and a late-arriving flight to dazzle Raptors evaluators. They had also been impressed by his background check. "He was squeaky clean," one Raptor official told the Toronto *Sun*. "He's something special and he has the potential to be someone special on the court as well."

That comment proved to be prophetic. Carter's transition to the NBA seemed almost seamless. "I had the luxury of being around a lot of NBA players in my experience at North Carolina," he explains. "I had the opportunity to talk to a lot of guys and they well prepared me on the ins and outs of the NBA — guys like Kenny Smith, Jerry Stackhouse, Rasheed Wallace, Hubert Davis … So nothing really surprised me because I had learned how to handle it." And from Day 1 in Toronto, Carter has been a superb acquisition, bringing on-court excitement and an engaging personality to a franchise that was in dire need of both.

The season before Carter arrived, Toronto had lost its first-ever Rookie of the Year, point guard Damon Stoudamire. Like many NBA players, Stoudamire had seemed less than enamored by the idea of spending his entire career in a Canadian city, particularly after the departure of Raptors Vice-President Isiah Thomas. The Raptors had been forced to deal their star point or risk losing him for nothing as a free agent. Waving goodbye to Stoudamire as a 16-win season came to a close had done absolutely nothing for fan confidence in Toronto. The refreshing arrival of Vince Carter couldn't have come at a better time, with the Raptors needing a boost to overcome the negativity surrounding the franchise and a solid gate attraction to help fill the near-completed Air Canada Centre.

Carter would fit both bills. He began his NBA career solidly with a 16-point effort in a 103–92 opening-night win in Boston and got better as the season progressed. He finished the year scoring 18.3 points per game and averaging 5.7 rebounds, 3.0 assists, 1.54 blocks and 1.10 steals. More important, his awe-inspiring dunks became a staple of late-night sportscasts across North America. Carter's flight patterns to the hoop were more than simply impressive; they were downright spectacular. "You go see this young man do his thing in the air and you leave Air Canada Centre talking about him and you want to go back and see him again. It's that simple," wrote Toronto *Star* columnist Dave Perkins.

Carter's raw athletic ability, imagination on his dunks, size, position and college background left plenty of people making the obvious comparisons. With Michael Jordan in retirement, people were openly suggesting that perhaps Vince Carter was the second coming, something that he good-naturedly played down. But another similarity between Carter and Jordan was becoming evident around the NBA. Those who looked past the sizzle of the slam dunks saw a complete basketball player in Vince Carter. For instance, his field goal percentage of .450 was the best on the team. He finished the 50-game season with 77 blocked shots, the highest for any non-centre or power forward and 16th in the league overall. "I think I have a lot of aspects to my game," Carter told reporters as his rookie season progressed. "It is going to take time to get noticed — I like to play defence and block shots if I can."

"He's more than just a jumper, although that over-shadows the other things," Jamal Mashburn told *Sports Illustrated.* " The real basketball fan, the purist, knows Carter is fundamentally sound. He can play. That high-light reel stuff is a disservice to him."

There were plenty of nights in the 1998–99 season, though, when Carter's highlight reel stuff was a thing of beauty. Like the time he threw down a monster dunk over six-foot-ten defensive stopper Alonzo Mourning, or the time he jammed on the head of 7–2 shot blocker Dikembe Mutombo. Or the night in Auburn Hills, Michigan, when he scored 17 fourth-quarter points, including the winner, to lead the Raptors to a 103–101 victory over the Detroit Pistons. Or the February chris-tening of the Air Canada Centre, when Carter scored the building's first-ever basket on a thundering one-handed alley-oop jam and finished with 27 points, six rebounds and five assists in a romp over the Grizzlies.

There were many memorable flight patterns over and around the hoop in Carter's rookie season, but the greatest reward for Raptors fans was that Carter's spec-tacular success came within the framework of a relatively successful team. The Raptors defied all doomsday pre-dictions, finishing with a 23–27 record and coming tan-talizingly close to the first-ever playoff berth for the fran-chise. "I guarantee we're gonna be (in the playoffs) next year," Carter told fans, throwing two pairs of his Puma shoes into the Air Canada Centre crowd following the Raptors' 96–87 season-ending win over Cleveland. "I'd like to thank everyone for a wonderful season."

Carter's high-wire act has created a buzz around basketball in Toronto, where the Raptors averaged more than 17,500 fans in 1999. And according to Toronto *Star* columnist Chris Young, Carter deserves the lion's share of the credit for making the NBA viable again in Canada. Best of all, Carter actually likes Toronto and has said on several occasions that he hopes to play his entire career in Canada. He seems genuinely enthused about a city whose basketball crowds were transformed from "like being at a bingo game or something" into a loud, raucous homecourt advantage. And instead of resting on his laurels, he ended his rookie NBA flight talking about his need to improve as a ballhandler, outside shooter and vocal leader in the Raptors' dressing room. "He has brought respect back to a franchise that people thought was on the brink of no return," Toronto coach Butch Carter (no relation) told the Toronto *Sun.* "He has been outstanding as an individual and has shown great character under a very stressful situation."

"You don't find many rookies like Vince," added teammate Charles Oakley. "He's in a different class. He wants to be a team player. He wants to work hard and get better. The way he carried himself and brought respect to Toronto around the NBA says a lot about him."

The way he carried himself also led to league-wide recognition for Vince Carter. In May, he was named the NBA's Rookie of the Year. Carter had received 113 of a possible 118 votes for the award. This was the third-highest total of the decade, behind only Tim Duncan and Shaquille O'Neal. The award certainly didn't shock anybody around the NBA. Carter had clearly been at the top of a solid rookie class that included point guards Mike Bibby of Vancouver and Jason Williams of Sacramento and Boston forward Paul Pierce. But after scanning the list of previous winners, which includes league legends Larry Bird, Michael Jordan and Patrick Ewing, Carter had to admit the award meant an awful lot. "I can't say I'm surprised," Carter told the press conference as he accepted the Gottlieb trophy. "But I'm overjoyed. This is a great honour. I looked at all the great players who have won the award and it's going to be tough to live up to the things they have brought to their organizations and basketball cities. But I'm going to try my hardest — try to have a great career and do a lot of great things for the Toronto Raptors."

At just 22, Vince Carter is already well on his way to accomplishing those goals. Besides being named top rookie, he was selected as the Central Division winner, and one of four league finalists for the 1999 NBA Sportsmanship Award. The award honours a player who best represents the ideals of sportsmanship on the court. Joining Carter as nominees were Eric Snow of Philadelphia, Kevin Garnett of Minnesota and the winner, Hersey Hawkins of Seattle.

"Vince is determined to have fun," his mother told the Hartford *Courant*. "He'll do everything he can to beat you, but he'll make sure he has fun doing it. I think it's true you have to have tenacity and desire to win, but I don't think that means you have to throw elbows, use profanity or abuse the officials. And I hope my son never stoops to that. If that's what it takes, then I would hope he changes careers."

Obviously, Michelle Carter-Robinson is not about to abdicate her role as a parent just because her son Vince is now a big-time NBA star. When Vince entered North Carolina, his mother made him promise that he would graduate. When he opted to enter the draft early, she held him to that verbal agreement. So, between his rookie and sophomore seasons in the NBA, Carter was back at Chapel Hill taking summer classes toward a degree in African-American studies. When the lockout put the brakes on his immediate jump into the NBA, Mom was there to encourage him not to let his routine — one that included 1,000 shots a day — slide.

Despite the fact Carter now plays in Toronto, his parents remain active in his life. They drove to Miami for his first NBA game in the state of Florida and they were on hand when the Raptors opened the Air Canada Centre in Toronto. His mother attended about 15 Toronto games in his rookie year and she plays a major role in Vince's Embassy of Hope, a charitable foundation that helps children and families. Michelle and Harry are also never more than a phone call away when Carter needs advice or somebody to talk to. They are, as Vince has said, "my motivators."

On a recent NBA Internet chat with fans, Carter was asked what his career inspiration had been. "It has to be my parents," he replied. "Believe it or not, they're my personal coaches. After every game I call them and get their take on how I played. They've been there since day one."

And they will continue to be there, despite the fact that Vince is already a millionaire and figures to sign a contract extension which will pay him more than $71 million U.S. over six years. His mother says he still has to take out the garbage and keep his room clean when he's at home. "We don't adore Vince as an NBA player," she told the *National Post*. "In a lot of homes, parents waive rights to be parents because now Junior is paying the bills," she adds. "I don't care how much money he has, I'm still his mother. The money doesn't change that."

That type of support and guidance has helped Carter reach his current status and given him the potential to climb much further. It's a support system that not every NBA player enjoys. And as he accepted the Rookie of the Year award on that May day, Vince Carter happily acknowledged as much. "My parents have always been around me. It's a tradition," Carter told the Toronto *Sun*. "They've always been in the crowd supporting me.

They've been a big factor in my life and always have been involved in my decision process. In the end, they've always allowed me to make up my own mind."

"It's kind of unfair when people make judgments about some (athletes) who have trouble being outstanding young men," Michelle Carter-Robinson says. "For some it is a tremendous leap without the support system. For Vince, it was a little hop."

CLASSIC CARTER

Name: Vincent (Vince) Lamar Carter
Nicknames: "Air Canada"; "UFO"; "The Pilot"
Position: Guard/Forward, Toronto Raptors
Born: January 26, 1977; Daytona Beach, FL
Height: 6'7"   **Weight:** 215 lbs.
High school: Daytona Beach Mainland, Daytona Beach, FL
College: University of North Carolina, Chapel Hill, NC
Drafted: 1998, No. 5 overall by Golden State Warriors; rights traded to Toronto Raptors

COLLEGE
As a freshman (1995–96)
31 games; 555 total minutes; .492 from field; .345 from three-point range; .689 from free-throw line; 119 total rebounds; 3.8 rebounds per game; 40 total assists; 1.3 assists per game; 232 total points; 7.5 points per game.
As a sophomore (1996–97)
34 games; 937 total minutes; .525 from field; .355 from three-point range; .750 from free-throw line; 152 total rebounds; 4.5 rebounds per game; 83 total assists; 2.4 assists per game; 443 total points; 13.0 points per game.
As a junior (1997–98)
38 games; 1,185 total minutes; .591 from field; .411 from three-point range; .680 from free-throw line; 195 total rebounds; 5.1 rebounds per game; 74 total assists; 1.9 assists per game; 592 total points; 15.6 points per game.

College career (1995-98)

103 games; 2,677 total minutes; .547 from field; .375 from three-point range; .705 from free-throw line; 466 total rebounds; 4.5 rebounds per game; 197 total assists; 1.9 assists per game; 1,267 total points; 12.3 points per game.

College honours

1995 — Member of USA Basketball junior team to world championships.

1997-98 — Associated Press Second Team All-American; The Sporting News Second Team All-American; All-ACC First Team; John Wooden Award candidate.

1997 and '98 — NCAA Tournament All-East Regional team.

NBA

1998-99 (Raptors)

50 games; 49 games started; 1,760 total minutes; 35.2 minutes per game; .450 from field; .288 from three-point range; .761 from free-throw line; 283 total rebounds; 5.7 rebounds per game; 149 total assists; 3.0 assists per game; 77 blocks; 55 steals; 913 total points; 18.3 points per game.

NBA honours

1998-99 — NBA Rookie of the Year; NBA All-Rookie First Team; NBA Sportsmanship Award, Central Division Winner

Sources

Toronto *Sun*

National Post

Globe and Mail

Toronto *Star*

Hartford *Courant*

Canadian Press

Associated Press

Sports Illustrated

Fox Sports

ESPN

Official NBA Register, (regular-season) Guide and Draft Media Guide

NBA.com

TIM DUNCAN

It was the kind of question a college basketball coach asks a thousand times during his career. Most of the time, these questions turn up nothing. This one would unearth a Caribbean gem.

In late August of 1992, head coach Dave Odom was sitting in his office at Wake Forest University when one of his former players, Chris King, dropped in for a quick visit. King had recently been drafted by the Seattle SuperSonics. With some other incoming NBA rookies, he had just returned from a brief playing tour of the Caribbean. (At the time, the NBA made a habit of sending its fresh talent on goodwill tours to areas not normally exposed to professional basketball.)

"How'd you enjoy your trip, Chris?" Odom greeted his former player. "Did you see anybody we ought to be interested in?"

"Well, actually coach, I did," King replied.

The former Wake Forest forward explained that he had noticed a 16-year-old on one of the islands who stood about six-foot-ten. Despite his tender age and rather remote home, this teenage prospect had fared surprisingly well against King's tourmate, NBA big man Alonzo Mourning, in one of the exhibition games.

Dave Odom was immediately intrigued.

"What's this kid's name?" the coach asked King.

"I don't know."

"What island is he on?" Odom continued.

"I don't know."

"This kid is six-ten and can play, and you don't remember his name or what island he lives on?" said Odom, shaking his head.

The mystery didn't last long. Odom quickly assigned his lead recruiter, Wake Forest assistant Larry Davis, to the case. Within a couple of days, the basketball office had a name, an island and even a high school for this exotic prospect.

The prospect was Tim Duncan, a 16-year-old who lived on St. Croix in the U.S. Virgin Islands. Little did Dave Odom or Chris King know that, seven years later, this unknown kid from the remote island would evolve into the dominant player in the NBA.

Ironically, Tim Duncan might have never thought seriously about basketball had it not been for the events in his life in 1989. As a youngster, he had been a competitive swimmer with dreams of following the lead of his older sister, Tricia, who had represented the Virgin Islands in the 1988 Seoul Olympics. By his early teens, Duncan was a nationally ranked 400-metre freestyler in his age group.

But 1989-1990 brought sadness and destruction into the life of teenage Tim Duncan. Just a day before his 14th birthday his mother, Ione, succumbed to breast cancer. A few months before, Hurricane Hugo had devastated the islands, forever altering Duncan's path. The storm's 135-mile-an-hour winds lashed St. Croix with a brutal vengeance, destroying the swimming pool in which Duncan had trained. The gangly youngster was left with a choice — either train in the ocean, where he was understandably nervous about sharks, or find a new sport.

Tim Duncan decided to switch his focus. First, he took up football and then, as a ninth-grader, settled seriously on basketball. The choice was a wise one. As Duncan grew rapidly through junior high and high school, he overcame the clumsy teen stage and eventually emerged as the dominant high school player for his school, St. Dunstan's Episcopal.

Tim Duncan was well on his way to becoming the dominant high school player on the Virgin Islands by the time Wake Forest University was interested in him. But it's a big jump from the islands to the gyms of the mainland U.S. Even though Dave Odom had heard good things about the kid from St. Croix, he knew he had to see this player with his own eyes.

Two days before the National Collegiate Athletic Association (NCAA) fall recruiting period ended in 1992, Odom boarded a flight for Tim Duncan's home. The Virgin Islands are a collection of Caribbean islands south of the Bahamas and north of Haiti that consist of about 165 square miles. On a spectacular Sunday morning, Odom landed on sunny St. Croix, a tranquil spot known for its pristine white-sand beaches and delightfully warm climate. Tim Duncan was there to meet Odom at the airport. That impressed the coach, who noticed immediately that the lanky youngster had mature personal skills for his age and was unaffected by the recruiting scene which seemed to spoil so many American players. He had no attitude, no expectations. "He wasn't tarnished," Odom says now.

The other thing the veteran Wake Forest head coach noticed right away was that Tim Duncan was *actually* six-foot-ten, not shorter, as so many prospects turned out to be when he finally saw them in person.

But Odom had really come to see Duncan play basketball. And the game that Sunday, a regular fixture on the island, was to be played outdoors. "Coach, come at 4 p.m." Duncan told him. "There's a court where everybody plays."

"Tim, what if it rains?" Odom asked.

"Coach, if it rains, we won't play."

A few hours later, Dave Odom arrived at the picturesque court, which was located oceanside and adjacent to a grassy knoll. On the asphalt, players of all ages gathered for a massive pickup game. Odom felt like the only white face in the crowd of about 200 gathered to watch. This seaside scene was certainly different from the high school gyms and arenas where he normally scouted prep prospects. "It was the way recruiting ought to be done," the coach laughs now.

Odom found a seat and waited for the action to begin. He was surprised when Duncan didn't play in the day's first pick-up game. But the youngster quickly explained to him that if he played in the first game, he would be placed on an inferior team by the other players and wouldn't be able to stay on the court as long. "I'll wait until the second game and choose my own team," he explained. "Then you'll be able to see me play longer."

"Right away," Odom recalls, "I was impressed by his ability to think ahead, well beyond his years." The Wake Forest coach was also impressed with Duncan's skills. They were undeveloped and unharnessed but, combined with his height, they held undeniable promise. For a big player, he was athletic and he had a nice touch with the ball. "He was a diamond in the rough," Odom says.

When the games were finished, Duncan approached Odom. "Coach, did you see enough?" asked the youngster. Odom already knew the kid could jump and run and think well enough to be a terrific player. All he wanted to see now was a turnaround jumper and a jump hook. Duncan took the ball onto the court and performed those moves. The jump hook he displayed was virtually the same one Duncan now uses in the NBA. Watching this, Odom knew it was just a matter of refining these weapons and then teaching this obviously bright young man how and when to use them.

"That's it," the coach said. "I've seen all I need to see."

Wake Forest wasn't the only school to visit Tim Duncan on St. Croix. The honour-roll student was also visited by Providence, Delaware, Georgetown and Hartford. And Duncan took a handful of recruiting trips to the mainland. But in mid-February, after visiting Wake Forest's Winston-Salem, North Carolina campus, he committed to the Atlantic Coast Conference (ACC) school. "It was very, very easy," Odom says now of the process of landing the biggest recruit of his coaching career. "It's really a study in contrasts (when compared to the traditional American recruiting process)."

Tim Duncan had already received some minor exposure to mainland U.S. basketball when, as a young high-schooler, he had visited his sister in Columbus, Ohio and had attended the Ohio State summer camp. At the time, he had gone virtually unnoticed by U.S. college coaches combing for emerging talent. When he arrived at Wake Forest's campus in the fall of 1993, ready to play for the Demon Deacons, Duncan was no longer an unknown prospect. But neither was he among the best-known freshmen coming into the NCAA. In fact, he was considered the school's third best recruit that season.

That would quickly change.

"Tim had a good feel for fundamentals, but they were natural fundamentals," Odom says now. "He

needed direction." Duncan took that direction extremely
well. The coaching staff at Wake Forest found him to be
a sponge for information and technique. Everything a
coach told him sunk in. He accepted instruction and
then worked diligently to perfect the lessons, applying
the same individual work ethic he had honed as a young
competitive swimmer.

Still, despite his height, talent and hard work, the
jump from St. Croix hoops to the ACC — one of the
top college leagues in the U.S. — was a sizable one.
Because of injuries to other players, he was a starter for
the Demon Deacons as a freshman. In his first outing, a
national TV overtime loss to the host team in the Great
Alaskan Shootout, he was held scoreless while grabbing
six rebounds and blocking three shots. "He absolutely
started at the bottom," Odom recalls, "but he just got
better and better."

"I'd never played in that level of competition coming out of the Virgin Islands," Duncan says now. "But
luckily I had time to kind of get into it and I walked
into a great situation (at Wake Forest). It gave me an
opportunity to play a lot and really get used to it quickly."
The adjustment process certainly didn't seem to take
long. Despite the enormous leap into the pressure-
packed, highly athletic world of the ACC, where college basketball is almost a religion, Duncan averaged
more than 30 minutes a game as a freshman, posting
close to a double-double (9.8 points and 9.6 assists) per
outing. But it was during his sophomore season that his
career, and potential future as an NBA great, really came
into focus. Duncan would average 16.8 points, shoot
.591 from the field, pull down 12.5 rebounds and average more than two assists per game. As his second year
in the NCAA came to a close, scouts were already whis-
pering that if Duncan declared himself eligible for the

1995 NBA draft, he would go No. 1 overall.

There was absolutely no doubt about Duncan's place in the pro game after his junior college season. He bumped up his scoring average to 19.1 and his assists total to nearly three per game and was named to *The Sporting News* All-America first team. By now, Duncan was everybody's No. 1 draft pick if he decided to leave school a year early. But remembering a promise to his mother that he would graduate from college, Duncan decided to bypass the instant big money and return to Wake Forest for his senior year.

Basketball fans at the school were overjoyed that Tim Duncan would remain in college at a time when underclassmen and even high school players were flooding the NBA. And Duncan himself had a rationale for his decision that was difficult to dispute. "Why should I try to do today what I'll be better prepared to do at sometime in the future?" he asked a reporter.

Duncan's senior season with the Demon Deacons was a fitting cap to his college career. He averaged 20.8 points on .608 shooting and pulled down an NCAA-best 14.7 rebounds while dishing out an average 3.2 assists. There was absolutely no doubt about who was the best prospect in college basketball. Tim Duncan was the *Sporting News,* Naismith and Wooden player of the year and he was everybody's first-team All-American. He was also the overwhelming consensus as the No. 1 pick in the 1997 NBA draft, a draft that scouts described as: "Tim Duncan and everybody else." And by delaying his entry into the league until after his senior season, he had inadvertently set himself up with a perfect situation in which to begin his pro career.

The bottom 13 teams in the NBA standings after each regular season are given first consideration in the league's annual June draft of college players. The teams with the absolute worst records are awarded the best chance in the draft lottery — the system used to determine which team picks first, second, third and so on. In Tim Duncan's draft year, the No. 1 pick was considered golden.

Normally, the No. 1 pick goes to a team in dire straits, a team which looks at the incoming player as a franchise saviour. Ironically, however, in 1997 it was the San Antonio Spurs who had the chance to select Duncan. In the previous season, the Spurs had sunk nearly to the bottom of the Midwest Division standings after their all-star centre, David Robinson, suffered a back injury that sidelined him for all but six games. Robinson's absence resulted in the Spurs sliding from division champions all the way to second last in the Midwest. At season's end, they had posted just 20 wins against 62 losses. Their miserable record had a massive silver lining, however: the right to pick Tim Duncan in the draft. They would be able to add the best player in college basketball to their frontcourt, to team up with a healthy and returning Robinson.

The situation was also a terrific one for Duncan. Instead of going to a perennial loser, where the pressure would be immense to produce immediately, Duncan became part of a team that figured to be a solid playoff contender. And as Spurs' coach and general manager Gregg Popovich would find out quickly, the newcomer fit right in. "He was a really well-prepared rookie," Popovich says, recalling Duncan's first training camp. "Coach Odom and his staff did a great job with him at Wake Forest. I mean, his footwork was great in the post. He understood how to play the game. He just more or less had to get initiated to the pro game and learn how to play the four (power forward) position and that sort of thing. But he came really fundamentally prepared from the work he did at Wake Forest."

That preparation was evident immediately when Duncan hit the floor with some of the Spurs for summer workouts in Aspen, Colorado, a few weeks after the draft. In camp, Popovich matched up the rookie against David Robinson. And although he was butting heads against the 1995 league MVP and a player voted as one of the NBA's 50 all-time greatest, Duncan held his own. In fact, he did more than that. On many occasions, he surprised the Spurs and their coaching staff by getting the better of the veteran. Robinson had long been known as a tremendous defender. Now a rookie right out of college was scoring on him with some regularity. Veteran Spurs point guard Avery Johnson was immediately struck by how well Tim Duncan stood up to the challenge. "Tim really got the best of Dave like I've never really seen before," Johnson says now. "And so I knew right then and there ... I was like: 'We've got something special'."

Robinson, who had made a huge first impression himself when he'd come to San Antonio out of the U.S. Naval Academy eight years earlier, was also a little surprised. Soon after scrimmaging with Duncan, he was telling people that Duncan could already do some things that he couldn't. "I got a chance to play with him during the summer (prior to his rookie season)," Robinson says now. "That was the first time I really got a chance to go up close and personal with him. I was just very impressed with his attitude, his composure, his low-block stuff — hooks and all that. I mean, I had played against him in international competition, but that was brief. He had a good game but I wasn't that impressed. But when I saw him up close, man, saw how long he is, those big old hands, him not afraid of anybody or anything — you know, I was impressed."

Still, the adjustment to a longer schedule proved a challenge, even if it didn't seem so to outsiders. "I think the physical aspect of the NBA is the biggest part of what you've got to get used to, just because there are so many games on so many nights," Duncan says of the transition from college. "And then you've got to get used to the NBA game because it's a much different game than what you're used to in college. It is real tough, because you come in here out of college feeling pretty good and thinking you know a lot and you've got to kind of start over because it's a totally different game. And you've got to find what works and find your niche."

Nevertheless, the transition appeared relatively seamless for Tim Duncan. He entered his first training camp strongly and hasn't looked back. In the 1997–98 season, he justified the NBA scouts' drooling by playing a huge role in the Spurs' rebound to second place in the Midwest Division. After winning 20 games the previous season, the Spurs, with Duncan and Robinson as their "Texas Twin Towers," rolled up 56 victories, finishing second in their division to Utah. It was the biggest single-season turnaround in NBA history.

Duncan's numbers for his rookie season were quietly spectacular. He averaged 21.1 points, 11.9 rebounds and 2.7 assists, and shot .549 from the field. He was the only rookie selected for the league's mid-season All-Star Game and he was a near-unanimous choice as NBA Rookie of the Year, sweeping all six monthly ballots and receiving 113 of 116 year-end votes. Duncan was a force on both sides of the ball, racking up 206 blocks and earning a spot on the league's all-defensive squad. He also became only the ninth rookie to ever to make first-team All-NBA. "I have seen the future and it wears number 21," Houston Rockets forward Charles Barkley would say of the Spurs' young prize.

The only drawback to a phenomenal rookie season was San Antonio's relatively early ouster from the postseason. They were eliminated in five games by Utah in the second round. Still, Duncan managed to average 20.7 points and nine rebounds over his first nine postseason games. In his first-ever playoff game, he scored on seven straight fourth-quarter possessions to key a victory over the Phoenix Suns. His rookie year left San Antonio fans salivating in anticipation of things to come. They wouldn't be disappointed. There would be no sophomore jinx for Tim Duncan in the NBA. Quite the opposite, in fact.

After enduring the labour lockout that would cut the 1998–99 season to just 50 games and reduce his own future earnings by untold millions, Duncan resumed his career right where he'd left off. In fact, in many ways he improved. During his second season, he upped his scoring average to 21.7 points per game (sixth-best in the league) and once again earned All-NBA First Team as well as All-Defensive First Team honours. Duncan even finished third in voting for the league's Most Valuable Player award. He was also the only player in the league to crack the top 10 in five major statistical categories — including fifth in rebounding (11.4 per game) and seventh in blocks (2.52) — and he led the NBA in double-doubles with 37. By the time the regular season was over, observers around the league were generally agreeing that, in only his second year, Duncan was approaching the status of No. 1 player in the NBA.

"He's improved in a lot of areas," said Spurs' coach Gregg Popovich as the season wound down. "He's handled double-teams better. He plays better defence at the four position. He knows when to take over games and how to do it. So, he's improved in a lot of ways this year."

"We knew when we drafted him that he was a great college player," added former Spurs' seven-footer Will Perdue. "But there's always that word 'potential.' That's dangerous when you label a guy like that. But he's done more in the last two years than a lot of guys have done their whole career. I mean, he works on something in practice once and immediately puts it in his game. And it's just been really surprising the way he's kind of (gone from) rookie to now the main focus of our offence."

While Duncan's fundamentals and his consistency are now universally lauded across the league, there are those who feel he lacks personality. He has been mildly criticized for not showing more passion on the court. Instead, what fans see is a player who coolly makes a good thing happen and then forgets about it, a young man who isn't overly impressed with himself. Because he plays without exaggerated displays of emotion and without the tongue-wagging or trash-talking shown by many players of his generation, he has been categorized by some as boring or lacking fire. In his college days, rival fans at Duke would chant, "Spock! Spock!" comparing Duncan with the alien from *Star Trek* who was incapable of feeling emotions. His pro coach, Gregg Popovich, has said that Duncan is "on island time" and that he has an unusually even-keeled personality, never blowing things out of proportion. But perhaps Popovich put it best when he said Duncan has "no MTV in him at all."

In a May 7, 1999, article in *The Sporting News,* Duncan's considerable skills were listed in detail, but they were also followed by this comment: "Perhaps his biggest drawback is his personality. Publicly, at least, he doesn't have one." Teammates on the Spurs would disagree. They say Duncan is a person who likes his space but they also describe him as fun-loving and a practical joker. He just doesn't wear his emotions on his jersey.

"Well, he's quiet to the media. I would say that. But around me he's one of the craziest guys I've ever met," says guard Antonio Daniels, who entered the league the same year as Duncan and who is one of his closest friends on the Spurs. "Around me, he just lets it all flow because that's the type of relationship we have with one another," Daniels adds. "But you know, you can't be like that with everyone. He's not a flashy guy. He'll come to the game in some jeans and a pair of Nike boots, you know, not a suit and so forth. He's his own person and I think you have to respect that."

Instead of being a player who will raise his outstretched palms to the fans in an attempt to get them to raise the roof, or pull his jersey to one side and thump his chest to display that he's all heart, Tim Duncan is more likely to talk quietly to himself or to flash a wide-eyed expression on the court. These are not gestures that fit easily into nightly highlight reels. And neither do all his best plays on the basketball court. His terrific footwork and solid fundamentals, combined with his tall body, make the often difficult plays he makes appear easy. Ask a sportscaster to choose between showing a classically efficient Duncan bank shot or a Kobe Bryant 360-degree slam and the choice is an easy one.

"The one thing that he won't be, I don't think, is a guy who will carry this league, because he's not a guard, he's not flashy," offers his former San Antonio teammate Perdue, who won three championship rings in Chicago with Michael Jordan, the player who most recently "carried" the NBA. "Tim just goes out, he gets the job done. He doesn't talk to other people. He doesn't talk to the camera. He doesn't pump his fists in the air. And yet he leads by example. And nights when he's really on top of his game, it's something beautiful to watch …"

Coaches certainly find Duncan's fundamentally

sound game a thing of beauty. "Tim Duncan is unique," Philadelphia 76ers and U.S. Dream Team coach Larry Brown told the Lakeland, Florida *Ledger.* "I don't know how many guys come into our league with that type of ability and personality. He's unbelievable. He has no ego. He just wants to enjoy playing, enjoy the people he's around and do the best he can, and that's pretty good."

Duncan is hardly a bland drone, either. He has a knife collection that includes a three-foot Samurai sword, he likes video games and rap and hip-hop music, he sports tattoos of a magician and a wizard, and he makes a habit of wearing his practice shorts backwards for good luck. In a rollicking self analysis done for the March 1999 issue of *Sport Magazine,* he offered some interesting insight into the man behind the mask. Entitled "The Psychoanalysis of Tim Duncan, by Tim Duncan," the story began like this:

"For this story, the good people over at *Sport* asked me to psychoanalyze myself. So as I lay here on my comfortable couch at home, I thought it was time that I reveal who the real Tim Duncan was … OK, here goes: I've got a million things going on in my head at all times. There … I said it. If you ever see me and think I'm being stand-offish, please forgive me … in these moments, I am doing nothing but thinking. Sometimes thinking about nothing. That is why I am a quiet person by nature. After all, it is difficult to think while talking …"

"You ever see the movie *Good Will Hunting* starring Matt Damon?" Duncan added. "That's probably the best way to get a true psychoanalytical picture of me. I am just a taller, slightly less hyperactive version of the Damon character in that movie. I just enjoyed how he probed people and found out their weaknesses — what they liked and didn't like — just by asking questions and saying outlandish random stuff, just to get a reaction. People expect me to be this shy, quiet type, so I'll ask them outlandish questions in a serious tone many times just to get a reaction …"

Duncan explained how his approach also works to his advantage on the court. "I try to take this mentally probing attitude on the court with me at all times. People in college thought I was lackadaisical because I didn't show emotion. They thought I was soft because I didn't yell with every rebound. Emotions must not always be shown. If you show excitement, then you may also show disappointment or frustration. If your opponent picks up on this frustration, you are at a disadvantage. I made sure my opponents didn't know what was going on in my head — I guess that's why the fans never knew, either. Basketball is like a chess game: You cannot reveal all that you are thinking or you will be at a sizable disadvantage to your opponent."

Tim Duncan certainly seemed one mental and physical step ahead of his opponents as the 1999 playoffs wore on. He was a dominant force as the Spurs survived a tough opening series against Minnesota before dispatching the Los Angeles Lakers and Portland Trail Blazers. Through that run, much was made of the backseat David Robinson had taken in the Spurs' offence. Certainly, Duncan had become the No. 1 offensive option — but, in truth, the two had combined into a terrific "Texas Twin Tower" attack. The Spurs began the regular season 6–8 as their two seven-footers struggled to mesh on the court. But once each player's role was worked out, the Spurs went on a tear, finishing the regular season on a 31–5 run.

While it seemed that Duncan dominated on the offensive end for the Spurs, while Robinson anchored the defence, Robinson also connected on his share of feathery jumpers and dunks while Duncan swatted nearly three shots a game on the Spurs' interior defence. The most refreshing thing was how two immense talents could work together without ego ruining the mix. Robinson saw his offensive numbers decline from 21.6 points per game to just 15.8 in the 1998–99 regular season. But he has said more than once that his new role is perhaps the one for which he was best suited all along. And he readily agrees that the arrival of Tim Duncan has pushed him as a basketball player. "Oh, no question," Robinson says. "He does some things that I can't do, but on the overall, I've still got to prove that I'm the better player than him every night. And that's good — that makes you work."

"We'll go as far as Tim and Dave take us," Perdue told the Dallas *Morning News* as the playoffs continued. "The two together are greater than Jordan."

That, of course, is a matter of opinion. But as the 1999 playoffs came to a close, there was no doubt that Duncan and Robinson were the most effective force in the NBA. With their twin towers behind them, the Spurs needed just five games to eliminate the New York Knicks in the championship series.

The Spurs' success created a stir back home on St. Croix. A huge billboard was raised near the airport, welcoming visitors to the "Home of Tim Duncan." And a large contingent of fans from the Virgin Islands flew to San Antonio to attend the opening of the NBA Finals and cheer on their national treasure. It became a colourful side-story for NBC, which devoted a major half-time feature to his upbringing. "It was a blessing for me to grow up there," Duncan told the network.

Meanwhile, San Antonio fans were also counting their blessings. Tim Duncan would finish as the dominant performer of the 1999 playoffs, averaging 23.2

points, 11.5 rebounds and 43.1 minutes per game. He set the tone early against the Knicks, with a commanding 33-point performance in Game 1. He also clinched the Spurs' first-ever NBA championship with a 31-point night as San Antonio edged the Knicks 78–77 in Game 5 at Madison Square Garden. Minutes after the championship was official, Tim Duncan could be seen on NBC holding up his own video camcorder, catching the Spurs' celebration on tape. "Just making records for myself," Duncan told reporters. "Just keeping it on tape. It's a blessing to get where I am now. It's a blessing to do what we did this year. There are no guarantees I'll ever get back, so I'm enjoying this team, documenting this time."

As his second year in the NBA came to a close, there was absolutely no doubt that Tim Duncan was the Finals MVP. "It's an incredible honour," he told the NBC cameras after accepting the award in the post-game celebration. "But all it means is people are going to keep going after you."

It also means that Duncan is the best in his profession. "He's the best player in the league, and I thought he deserved the (regular season) MVP award," Knicks forward and former college rival Marcus Camby told the New York *Times*. "Not only does he score but he rebounds exceptionally well, he blocks shots and he plays aggressively on defence. I'm just trying to get where he's at right now."

Duncan took his game a step further in the summer following his first NBA title. Just a week after beating the Knicks in the Garden, he suited up for the U.S. Dream Team and travelled to Puerto Rico, where he helped his team qualify for the 2000 Olympic Games in Sydney, Australia.

Does the journey he has made over the last six years

— from St. Croix to MVP, to U.S. Olympian — ever blow his mind? "I've had some time to get used to it," Duncan laughs. "But, yeah, if I really think about it, it really does."

DUNCAN DATA

Name: Timothy Theodore Duncan
Nicknames: "Cash Flow"; "The Big Easy"; "Magnum VI"
Position: Forward/Centre, San Antonio Spurs
Born: April 25, 1976; St.Croix, U.S. Virgin Islands
Height: 7'   **Weight:** 248 lbs.
High school: St. Dunstan's Episcopal, Christiansted, St. Croix, U.S. Virgin Islands
College: Wake Forest University, Winston-Salem, North Carolina
Drafted: 1997, No. 1 overall by San Antonio Spurs

COLLEGE
As a freshman (1993–94)
33 games; 997 total minutes; .545 from field; 1.0 (1 for 1) from three-point range; .745 from free-throw line; 317 total rebounds; 9.6 rebounds per game; 30 total assists; 0.9 assists per game; 323 total points; 9.8 points per game.
As a sophomore (1994–95)
32 games; 1,168 total minutes; .591 from field; .429 from three-point range; .742 from free-throw line; 401 total rebounds; 12.5 rebounds per game; 67 total assists; 2.1 assists per game; 537 total points; 16.8 points per game.
As a junior (1995–96)
32 games played; 1,190 minutes played; .555 from field; .304 from three-point range; .687 from free-throw line; 395 total rebounds; 12.3 rebounds per game; 93 total assists; 2.9 assists per game; 612 total points; 19.1 points per game.
As a senior (1996–97)
31 games played; 1,137 minutes played; .608 from field; .273 from three-point range; .636 from free-throw line; 457 total rebounds; 14.7 rebounds per game; 98 total assists; 3.2 assists per game; 645 total points; 20.8 points per game.

College career (1993–97)

128 games played; 4,492 minutes played; .577 from field; .321 from three-point range; .689 from free-throw line; 1,570 total rebounds; 12.3 rebounds per game; 288 total assists; 2.3 assists per game; 2,117 total points; 16.5 points per game.

College honours

1993–97 — *The Sporting News* College Player of the Year; Naismith Award; John Wooden Award; CBS Player of the Year: Chevrolet Player of the Year; National Association of Basketball Coaches (NABC) Player of the Year; NABC Defensive Player of the Year; two-time ACC Player of the Year; two-time First Team All-America; three-time First Team All-ACC.

College records

No. 1 shotblocker in ACC history; No. 2 shotblocker in NCAA history; No. 3 rebounder in ACC history.

NBA

1997–98 (Spurs)

82 games; 82 games started; 3,204 total minutes; 39.1 minutes per game; .549 from field; 0.00 from three-point range; .662 from free-throw line; 977 total rebounds; 11.9 rebounds per game; 224 total assists; 2.7 assists per game; 206 blocks; 55 steals; 1,731 total points; 21.1 points per game.

1998–99 (Spurs)

50 games; 50 games started; 1,963 total minutes; 39.3 minutes per game; .495 from field; .143 from three-point range; .690 from free-throw line; 571 total rebounds; 11.4 rebounds per game; 121 total assists; 2.4 assists per game; 126 blocks; 45 steals; 1,084 total points; 21.7 points per game.

Career to date (1997–99)

132 games; 132 games started; 5,167 total minutes; 39.1 minutes per game; .527 from field; .059 from three-point range; .674 from free-throw line; 1,548 total rebounds; 11.7 rebounds per game; 345 total assists; 2.6 assists per game; 332 blocks; 100 steals; 2,815 total points; 21.3 points per game.

Playoffs to date (1998 and '99)

26 games; 26 games started; 1,107 total minutes; 42.6 minutes per game; .514 from field; 0.00 from three-point range; .724 from free-throw line; 276 total rebounds; 10.6 rebounds per game; 65 assists; 2.5 assists per game; 68 blocks; 18 steals; 581

total points; 22.3 points per game.
NBA honours
1997–98 — NBA Rookie of the Year award; All-NBA First Team;
NBA All-Defensive Second Team; NBA All-Rookie First Team;
selected to 1998 All-Star game.
1998–99 — Third in NBA MVP balloting; All-NBA First Team; All-
NBA Defensive First Team; NBA Finals MVP; selected to USA
Basketball senior team for the 2000 Olympic Games qualifying
tournament.

Sources
Associated Press
Hoop Magazine
Vancouver *Province*
Vancouver *Sun*
San Antonio *Express-News*
Sport Magazine
Dallas *Morning News*
Los Angeles *Times*
New York *Times*
The Sporting News
Lakeland *Ledger*
ESPN
Wake Forest University men's basketball website
NBA.com
NBC Sports
SlamDuncan website
Official NBA Register, (regular-season) Guide and Draft Media Guide

KEVIN GARNETT

They sat in the bleachers at floor level — about 20 professional basketball experts — waiting to be convinced. Waiting for some kind of sign that what they were doing wasn't crazy. Coaches, general mangers and scouts from the NBA had gathered at the University of Illinois-Chicago fieldhouse ... for what? To check out a high school kid?

But this wasn't just *any* high school kid. This was "Da Kid."

Such was the beginning of Kevin Garnett's rapid ascension from high school prom to basketball's big leagues. Just a few weeks earlier, in May of 1995, the 19-year-old had boldly declared that he was planning to become the first high schooler in more than 20 years to leap straight into the NBA, bypassing college completely.

This workout, a private June session for representatives of the 13 draft lottery teams, was the kid's litmus test. The assembled NBA brains had been invited by Garnett's representative, Eric Fleisher. Some had entered the gym carrying a healthy degree of skepticism. They would leave with a considerably different perspective.

This kid was good. Too skinny, sure; too young, definitely. But he stood six-foot-eleven, and as he went through his drills, the scouts could see he had the kind of athletic ability and quickness normally possessed by players a half foot shorter. It was obvious the kid had terrific hand-eye co-ordination and a massive wingspan that, combined with his vertical leap, made his pro potential virtually limitless. "But more impressive," says Minnesota Timberwolves player personnel director Rob Babcock, "was the way he approached the workout." Babcock remembers the session vividly. "He had 100 percent enthusiasm and competitiveness. He was all by himself (except for Detroit Pistons assistant coach John Hammond, who was putting him through his workout) but there was no problem. He showed all this himself. Most guys can't do that. His enthusiasm is very special. It's not a put-on. That's the way he is."

Joining Babcock from the Timberwolves' brain trust were team vice-president Kevin McHale and general manger Flip Saunders. Like many others, they had been doubtful heading into the session. But no longer. "We had no idea we were going to take him in the first round," McHale would later tell *Sports Illustrated*. "I didn't even want to go see him. I thought it was a waste of time. Then we went, and Flip Saunders and I were in the car afterward and we just looked at each other. I said, 'Wow, we're going to pick a high school kid in the first round.' It was that obvious."

Garnett's workout had catapulted him from question mark to sure-fire lottery selection. What the assembled had witnessed was a player who, if he spent a season or two in college basketball, would likely become a No. 1 overall pick. But college basketball was not an option for Kevin Garnett. While in his senior year at Chicago's Farragut Academy, he had attempted more than once to pass the standard exams that would qualify him for university entrance and scholarships. He had not succeeded. He had, however, become a schoolboy legend on the hardwood. In fact, Garnett had already won prestigious Mr. Basketball awards in two different states and had been named the top prep player in the country by *USA Today.*

Kevin Garnett grew up in the Greenville, South Carolina, middle-class suburb of Mauldin, where he was known as a kid obsessed with basketball. When his step-father refused to allow a hoop in the family driveway, he simply went to nearby Springfield Park where he would play the game night and day.

At 12 years old, he was a gangly five-foot-ten kid with limited skills. But round-the-clock practice and a huge growth spurt changed that. By age 15, Garnett stood six-foot-seven and was suddenly the king of the neighborhood court. "All he did was talk about basket-ball," Baron "Bear" Franks, one of the older players who initially gave Garnett a rough ride, would later recall for the *Pioneer Press.* "And every time you saw him, he had a ball. Sun up, sun down. Up and down the street. All day long. This is a guy who would lay down at 3 a.m. and then be up at 9 a.m. to play ball. He would think everyone else had to get up, too. And whoever did get up to play with him played all day. I mean, I liked bas-ketball, too. But not like he did."

In the ninth grade, with the encouragement of a close friend and without the knowledge of his parents, Garnett went out for the freshman team at Mauldin High. He soon became a prep star who packed school gymnasiums. In his junior year at Mauldin, Garnett led the Mavericks to a 22–7 record, averaging 27 points, 17 rebounds and seven blocks to earn South Carolina Mr. Basketball honours and rocket to the top of every col-lege coach's recruiting list.

But an incident near the end of that year would change Kevin Garnett's life forever. A white student was injured during a fight at his school. Some witnesses later claimed the fight was racially motivated. Although Garnett has stated repeatedly that he was simply a by-stander, he was nevertheless one of five black students charged with "second-degree public lynching" in the incident. Later that day, the high school basketball star was handcuffed in class and taken to jail. Because he had never been in any previous trouble with the law, Garnett qualified for pre-trial intervention and the charges against him were eventually dropped. But the experience was enough for his mother, Shirley Irby, to know her son needed a change of scenery.

Garnett had previously met William Nelson, the coach at Chicago's Farragut Academy, during a Nike summer basketball camp. When Nelson found out about the talented youngster's troubles in Mauldin, he sug-gested Garnett relocate and play his senior high school season at Farragut. By the time school started again, the family was in Chicago.

Going from Mauldin, a sleepy bedroom commu-nity of 14,000 people, to the west side of Chicago was a shock for both Garnett and his family. Suddenly, they had to cope with a new world of gangs and crime on their doorstep. At Farragut, Kevin found himself a mi-nority in the largely Hispanic student body. Just getting to and from school was a challenge. He dealt daily with the dangerous streets of his neighbourhood, which in-cluded a gang whose leader was named Seven-Gun Marcello. "The 'hood's real. Nothing's fake," Garnett would later tell *USA Today.* "Nothing's fun. If you have ten Hispanic guys bothering you, throwing rocks and shooting guns, you think twice about trying to walk to school. I never want to go back to that. I learned a lot in the streets. I learned a lot I could've learned differently. It was a jungle. I never want to live like that."

Although it was a rough adjustment off the court,

Garnett blossomed as a senior hoop star with the Farragut Admirals in the tough Chicago Public League. He helped the Admirals to a 28–2 record and their first-ever city title, averaging 25.2 points, 17.9 rebounds, 6.7 assists and 6.5 blocks in his senior season. Farragut was *USA Today*'s third-ranked team in the nation. Garnett, meanwhile, was named that publication's national prep player of the year as well as Mr. Basketball for Illinois after leading Farragut into the state quarter-finals.

Although he had been a huge high school star in South Carolina, it was obvious to Garnett and everybody else that the move to Chicago had paid dividends for his game. As his high school career ended, he was named to *Parade Magazine*'s All-America First Team. He was also voted outstanding player of the prestigious McDonald's All-America Game after scoring 18 points, grabbing 11 rebounds, dishing out four assists and blocking three shots. "I felt I was always aggressive on the court, but when I got (to Chicago), I took it to another level," Garnett told the *Pioneer Press*. "I had to. Being there put the dog in me, made me more aggressive. Just a little sign of being scared or weak on the court will make people take advantage of you. I learned that. To this day, I haven't seen a kid from Chicago who didn't play strong. It's in their blood. I think some of that attitude rubbed off on me."

Coming out of Farragut, Kevin Garnett would have been considered a monumental prize for college recruiters. But try as he might, he couldn't achieve a passing score on his college entrance exams. So, after faring well against pros such as Scottie Pippen and Ron Harper in some of Chicago's toughest pickup and summer games, he decided to take the plunge. In May, he called a press conference at Farragut to declare himself eligible for the 1995 NBA draft. The reaction to his pronouncement

was predictable. Nobody thought it was a good idea.
No player had successfully made such a jump since 1975,
when Darryl Dawkins had risen from Maynard Evans
high school in Orlando. Few thought Garnett was ready
and fewer still were keen on the general concept of high
schoolers bypassing college to join the NBA. "No knock
on Mr. Garnett, but obviously we would prefer these
kids play college basketball, then join the league," NBA
deputy commissioner Russ Granik told reporters.

But Kevin Garnett's individual workout just weeks
before the draft changed the prevailing wisdom amongst
NBA insiders. They still might not be crazy about drafting high schoolers, but it was clear that this particular
high schooler was a special case. Between that June
workout, which occurred in conjunction with the NBA's
annual Chicago pre-draft camp, and the draft itself, a
huge buzz was building around Garnett.

That workout so impressed assembled scouts that,
suddenly, the story wasn't about high schooler Kevin
Garnett declaring for the draft but rather how high he
would go. The T-Wolves had made up their mind they
wanted him. Now they had to hope he would still be
around when they picked in the No. 5 spot in the June
28 draft at Toronto's SkyDome.

On the day of the draft, as he was preparing to head
to the Green Room, Kevin Garnett received a call from
his high school coach at Farragut. His latest college entrance exam results had come back. Ironically, he had
finally scored high enough to enter university. By now,
however, it was too late. There was no turning back.

As the 1995 draft opened, Golden State made Maryland forward Joe Smith the first pick, followed by Alabama forward Antonio McDyess to the Los Angeles
Clippers and North Carolina guard Jerry Stackhouse to
the Philadelphia 76ers. When Washington made Tar

Heel forward Rasheed Wallace the No. 4 selection, the Timberwolves knew they had Garnett. It was a huge gamble for the Minnesota franchise. In their six NBA seasons, the Timberwolves had been perennial losers, including four straight years of 60 or more losses. Now they were using a valuable lottery pick on a high school kid? There was bound to be some heavy second-guessing. But McHale and his staff were confident. In Kevin Garnett, they believed they were drafting a player who would have been a sure-fire No. 1 after a year or two of college. They were simply getting their prize early. "The only anxiety I had in the whole draft was when the fourth pick came up," McHale said afterward. "I'm sure glad Washington didn't say: 'Kevin Garnett.' Our pick was done the minute that Washington took Wallace. We knew who we were going to take. We're all very excited. We got the kid who we think maybe has the most talent in the draft. He is very young, but he is very talented."

The focus, or rather the obsession, of basketball fans would soon swing to just how very young Garnett was. He had long since become a major story around the league and even outside basketball circles. Prior to the draft, *Sports Illustrated* featured the teenage phenomenon on its cover with the headline: "Ready or Not …" Garnett himself seemed to have no doubts. "This is no easy step," he said, minutes after being drafted. "A lot of people said I really didn't think about this, but I did … If given the chance, I am going to prove to all of you that I am man enough to take what is given and mature enough to give it out." He then signed a three-year contract with the Timberwolves worth $5.6 million U.S. It was a world removed from the $100 per week he had earned during a summer job flipping burgers and cleaning washrooms at a South Carolina Burger King.

There was much talk before and after the draft about

easing the youngster's entry into the NBA. Toronto Raptors boss Isiah Thomas had even suggested that, if he was going to draft Garnett, he would consider playing the teenager only in home games and select road contests to begin with. The Timberwolves never considered that step, but they did look into the possibility of finding a local family for Garnett to live with, and arranging for him to meet and socialize with members of the University of Minnesota basketball team, something they felt would provide him with peers closer to his own age.

None of that was necessary, however. Garnett brought his closest friends from Mauldin and his family to live with him in Minneapolis. For the first season, his friends were allowed on road trips with the team. At Garnett's request, his agent put him on an allowance, keeping his expenditures modest with the exception of a Lexus. This was all the support system Kevin Garnett would need — this and the Sega video game system that accompanied him around the league. "That's what makes him happy," Babcock says. "He's not a partyer. He's a low-maintenance person. He was very professional (even as a rookie). He was unbelievable for his age."

Nevertheless, there were certanly some adjustments for Kevin Garnett. From the first day of training camp in St. Cloud, Minnesota, the rookie was tested by veterans such as Doug West and Sam Mitchell. The two-a-day workouts and the physical banging from older players took their toll on his still-developing body. But although he was skinny and quiet, from day one Garnett refused to let himself be pushed around. On the first day of camp, he got into a minor altercation with Mitchell. "I told myself, 'If I can get through this, I can get through anything'," Garnett confided to the Minneapolis *Star Tribune*.

There were plenty of curious people wondering if Garnett would get through this NBA initiation in one piece. Just a few months after graduating from high school, he was travelling across North America, a teenager among men. And not only that, in every NBA city he had become The Story. Every media swarm wanted to know how he was holding up to the routine, whether he regretted not going to college, what he did in his spare time. "I've been in a lot of mature situations, where I really had to fend for myself, where I had to take care of my own, take care of my family," Garnett told *XXL Basketball* magazine. "So what's so hard about getting a bundle of money and living, taking care of yourself? ... What's so hard about going from rags to riches?"

Rob Babcock, the Minnesota scout, believes that a high school basketball player may actually have to make more of a lifestyle adjustment going to college than to the pros. "There is a lot more stress on a kid going away to college than there is on a kid coming to the NBA," he says. "At college, you've got to decide where to live, line up your classes, take care of your homework and basketball. In the NBA, you worry about one thing — playing basketball. You don't have to worry about academics. The biggest challenge in the NBA is what to do with your spare time."

One question Garnett soon didn't have to answer was whether he belonged in the NBA. During his rookie season, he proved that he did. From the first day of training camp, he displayed an extraordinary grasp on the fundamentals for a player with no college experience. Among other things, he had the ability to watch a move and immediately adapt it into his game.

Things started slowly for the league's youngest rookie, however. Head coach Bill Blair didn't play Garnett much as the 1995–96 season began. That was reported to be one of the reasons Blair was fired by Kevin McHale and replaced by Flip Saunders just a quarter of the way into the schedule. Once Saunders took over on the bench, Garnett's playing time increased dramatically and so did his production. After averaging 19 minutes, six points, four rebounds and one block as a sub, he upped those averages to 37 minutes, 14 points, eight rebounds and two blocks over 43 games as a starter. It was obvious: The kid could play. "Kevin is the whole package," Kevin McHale would tell *Basketball America* as the season unfolded. "Put it this way — it was the easiest draft pick maybe I'll ever have. He already does things no one else can do."

Garnett's first professional start came January 9, 1996, at the Great Western Forum in Los Angeles. At 19 years and 235 days, he was the third youngest player ever to start an NBA game. By the end of the season, he would lead Minnesota in rebounding 23 times, and block a team-record 131 shots. Over the 82-game schedule — a schedule skeptics had felt would chew up a high school kid — Garnett had averaged 10.4 points, 6.3 rebounds and 28.7 minutes per game. He had also shot .491 percent from the field, recorded 12 double-doubles and already become the final Minnesota player announced during pre-game introductions at the Target Center, signalling his arrival as the focal point of the franchise. Through his infectious all-out exuberance and enthusiasm on the court, he had also captured the hearts of Minnesota fans.

That first season included an impressive eight-point, four-rebound, six-assist appearance in the Rookie All-Star Game at San Antonio, Texas. During All-Star Weekend, Flip Saunders handed Garnett a note that read: "Think where you were a year ago." Just one year earlier, Garnett had been a high school senior, watching the All-Star festivities in a Chicago apartment; now he was part of the show. And there were plenty of other rookie highlights — including a 33-point night in March against the Boston Celtics, and a 20-point, eight-rebound February "homecoming" in Chicago, when Garnett impressed opponents Michael Jordan and Scottie Pippen with a brilliant performance. "It's quite evident he made the right decision," Jordan would say, signifying that Garnett belonged. This Chicago breakthrough came despite the fact Garnett's former high school teammate, Ronnie Fields, had just two days earlier been seriously injured in an automobile accident. Garnett wore Fields' No. 23 and "Ronnie" written on his basketball shoes.

Meanwhile, there were lessons to be absorbed on the court, particularly at the defensive end, where Garnett was covering much quicker players than in high school. In October, Lakers forward Cedric Ceballos blew by the rookie for an easy hoop and then mouthed to the courtside fans at the Forum: "He's not ready." In another early-season game, Garnett was being embarrassed by Milwaukee's Glenn "Big Dog" Robinson to the point where he became frustrated, calling for the ball in order to get even with Robinson. Bill Blair pulled him from that game.

In November, as Garnett prepared to enter a home contest, he realized he wasn't wearing his jersey under his warm-up top. The rookie had to return to the locker room and retrieve it before going into the game, to much laughter from his older teammates. But Garnett also got plenty of support from the Minnesota dressing room. Sam Mitchell helped him adjust to the league and Garnett's teammates also endeavoured to include him. In Salt Lake City, Garnett was among a group of Timberwolves who went for a post-game meal at a licensed nightspot. When Garnett was told he couldn't be served because he was under-age, his teammates left with him. "I never felt like Kevin needed a mentor," Sam Mitchell would later tell *XXL Basketball* magazine. "You could tell after the first day, he was a man. He was a 19-year-old who had seen a lot and been through a lot. Kevin was a mature adult. He knew how to make mature choices. You could just tell. He was different from most 19-year-olds."

Not everybody was consistently generous to Garnett, however. Teammate Christian Laettner, who had been a T-Wolves' focal point before Garnett's arrival, ripped into the rookie during an interview following a February loss to Washington. "You've got to have the rookies and young kids shut up … We've got a lot of people who think they know everything," Laettner said, obviously targeting Garnett. The rookie responded in a mature manure that stunned management. "That's just one grown man's opinion," he said. Less than a week later, Laettner was traded to Atlanta, leaving little doubt that the Timberwolves were willing to put a total commitment behind Garnett. "The season was long, sort of confusing, sort of difficult," Garnett told the Minneapolis *Star Tribune* when it was over. "I learned a lot. I learned how to be as a person, which is just to be myself. A lot of people didn't think I'd make it. It just goes to show what they know."

Over the next three seasons, Garnett has erased any doubt about whether or not he'd "make it." Now the only question is how good he will eventually get. By the age of 22, he had completed four NBA seasons and played in two All-Star Games. At a time when most players are just getting out of college, he was already a seasoned veteran, while still developing physically. Although he is still listed at six-foot-eleven by the NBA, many

Prep-to-pro **Kobe Bryant** of the Lakers reaches around for a steal from the Grizzlies' **Shareef Abdur-Rahim**. (CP PICTURE ARCHIVE, NICK PROCAYLO)

Charismatic **Kobe Bryant** soars in for a slam against Vancouver. (DUOMO)

FACING PAGE, TOP: Grizzlies' **Shareef Abdur-Rahim** lines up a jumper as Raptors' **Vince Carter** attempts to draw the offensive foul. (CP PICTURE ARCHIVE, KEVIN FRAYER)

FACING PAGE, BOTTOM: **Vince Carter** gets airborne to make an assist as **Shareef Abdur-Rahim** defends. (CP PICTURE ARCHIVE, KEVIN FRAYER)

The New Jersey Nets are reduced to spectators as **Kobe Bryant** finishes with a fashionable dunk. (DUOMO, BERNSTEIN)

Los Angeles swingman **Kobe Bryant** tosses down a tasty one-hander against the Clippers. (SPORTSCHROME, BRIAN SPURLOCK)

SKYWALKING

Toronto's **Vince Carter** displays the mid-air ballet moves that made him 1999 NBA Rookie of the Year. (CP PICTURE ARCHIVE, KEVIN FRAYER)

FACING PAGE, TOP: San Antonio's **Tim Duncan** shows emotion skeptics felt he was lacking. (CP PICTURE ARCHIVE, NICK PROCAYLO)

FACING PAGE, BOTTOM: Twin Texas Towers **Tim Duncan** (right) and **David Robinson** celebrate their 1999 NBA championship. (CP PICTURE ARCHIVE, MARK LENNIHAN)

For opponents such as the Clippers, the
smooth **Tim Duncan** has proven to be
unstoppable. (SPORTSCHROME, MICHAEL ZITO)

Minnesota's **Kevin Garnett** has carved out a reputation for finishing with authority. (AP, BILL JANSCHA)

SKYWALKING

Few NBA players have the combination of size, reach, speed and agility of Timberwolves star **Kevin Garnett**. (AP, SCOTT TROYANOS)

FACING PAGE, TOP: Ever since coming into the NBA out of high school, **Kevin Garnett** has won over Minnesota fans with his exuberance. (DUOMO, DARREN CARROLL)

FACING PAGE, BOTTOM: **Kevin Garnett** displays the concentration that has made him a top offensive threat. (DUOMO, WILLIAM SALLAZ)

Washington's **Chamique Holdsclaw** displays the hops that separate her from most other players. (DUOMO, PAUL J. SUTTON)

FACING PAGE, TOP: Mystics star **Chamique Holdsclaw** follows through with her free-throw. (DUOMO, PAUL J. SUTTON)

FACING PAGE, BOTTOM: WNBA Rookie of the Year **Chamique Holdsclaw** elevates for a jumper. (DUOMO, PAUL J. SUTTON)

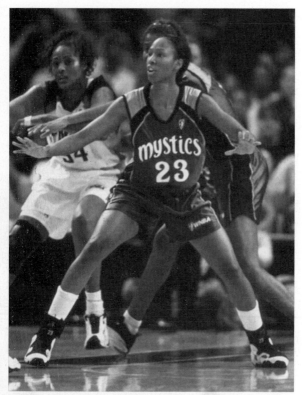

Mystics' **Chamique Holdsclaw** has the star power that the WNBA hopes will elevate women's pro basketball. (DUOMO, PAUL J. SUTTON)

S K Y W A L K I N G

In 1999, Philadelphia's **Allen Iverson** rose above the crowd to become the shortest player ever to capture the NBA scoring title. (DUOMO)

76ers super-guard **Allen Iverson** jumps to finish off a fast break.
(DUOMO)

FACING PAGE, TOP: Philadelphia's **Allen Iverson** drives around the
defence of the Lakers' Kobe Bryant. (DUOMO)

FACING PAGE, BOTTOM: **Allen Iverson** embraces **Ann Iverson**, his mother
and No. 1 fan. (AP WIDE WORLD PHOTOS, DAN LOH)

Allen Iverson and **Steve Nash** both became pros during the 1996 NBA Draft in East Rutherford, N.J. (CP PICTURE ARCHIVE, ANTHONY ONCHAK)

Steve Nash, directing traffic for Dallas, plans to be part of a Maverick turnaround. (AP WIDE WORLD PHOTOS, CHRIS MATULA)

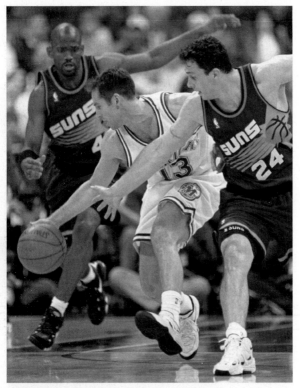

Mavericks point guard **Steve Nash** dribbles through a pair of
Phoenix Suns. (AP WIDE WORLD PHOTOS, TIM SHARP)

It has been a remarkable rise for Clippers centre **Michael Olowokandi** (right), shown here as a rookie against **David Robinson** of the Spurs. (SPORTSCHROME, MICHAEL ZITO)

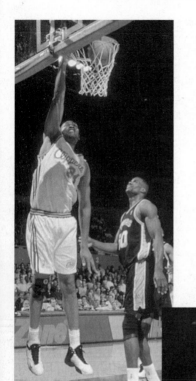

It took awhile for him to adjust to the NBA, but Clippers' big man **Michael Olowokandi** possesses size, athleticsm and the ability to overcome huge hurdles.
(SPORTSCHROME, MICHAEL ZITO)

Charlotte Sting pint-sized point guard **Dawn Staley** has a special place in pro basketball's land of the giants. (AP WIDE WORLD PHOTOS, CHUCK BURTON)

Charlotte's **Dawn Staley**: She can drive and dribble
with the best of the WNBA. (AP WIDE WORLD PHOTOS,
TOP: CHUCK BURTON; BOTTOM: NELL REDMOND)

observers believe that Garnett now stands closer to seven-foot-one. Those scouts who saw so much potential before the 1995 draft are now seeing that potential fulfilled. Quite simply, Kevin Garnett does things a seven-footer should not be able to do. He is capable of playing at least four positions on the floor. He is capable of dominating the best league in the world. And he is still learning just how dominant he can be. As *Star Tribune* writer Steve Aschburner once put it: "Watching Garnett discover himself on 29 courts throughout the league is what it must have been like to hear a young John Coltrane find his chops. Something special is happening here."

Since coming into the league, Garnett has rapidly ascended to the point where he is now considered to be one of the top five players in the NBA. He is also a key member of the USA Basketball Dream Team. His scoring and rebounding numbers have been on a constant rise, going from 10.4 points and 6.3 rebounds as a rookie, to 17.0 and 8.0 in Year 2, 18.5 and 9.6 in Year 3, and 20.8 and 10.4 in Year 4. As his fourth season concluded, Kevin Garnett was in the top 20 in six major NBA statistical categories. "He's getting better all the time, but he's still a young kid," Kevin McHale told CBS *SportsLine* late in the 1999 season. "There are times we forget he's 22. He's still maturing physically. His upside is tremendous, and he's still got a ways to go. That's the excitement about Kevin. As good as he is now, he'll get better." Not coincidentally, Garnett's arrival has also sparked a turnaround in the fortunes of the previously inept Timberwolves. Prior to the high school kid coming to Minneapolis, the team had never made the playoffs. Now they have been to the post-season three years running.

There have been disappointments for Garnett in Minnesota, however. Early in his career, he wondered what it would have been like to go to college like other players his age. And during the 1997–98 season, he endured a stretch when basketball wasn't as much fun anymore. "A lot of times I've been acting the way someone else wants me to act," he told the *Star Tribune*. "People tell me 'You don't act like most 21-year-olds.' Maybe I have to act like a kid, instead of a 30-year-old or 40-year-old. I need to do some soul searching. I need to find myself." A major setback in his young career came with the departure of longtime friend and on-court collaborator Stephon Marbury from Minnesota during the winter of 1999. The two had been close since high school and Garnett had been thrilled when the Timberwolves obtained Marbury out of Georgia Tech during the 1996 draft. But less than three years later, the flashy point guard forced a trade out of Minnesota to the New Jersey Nets, breaking up a combination that had given the Timberwolves one of the best one-two punches in the league. Garnett has soldiered on nonetheless. "There have been times when I've seen how it's worn on his face," Flip Saunders told the *Star Tribune*. "But he's a resilient young man, very mature beyond his age. He seems to always bounce back. Very rarely is he down, even if he *is* down."

Meanwhile, Kevin Garnett has also been influential in the financial restructuring of the NBA. Some called him "the poster boy" for the NBA's 1998–99 labour unrest when a lockout nearly killed an entire season. The reason? The mammoth contract extension that Garnett had signed in 1997. Garnett and his agent also incurred the wrath of Minnesota basketball fans by rejecting a $103.5-million U.S. offer from the Timberwolves. They then held out for the $126-million, six-year deal that served as a wake-up call for the entire league and prompted NBA owners to shut down their sport in search of more salary control. "Greed ... that's personified by Kevin Garnett," Utah Jazz owner Larry Miller told reporters, "but maybe even more by his agent, Eric Fleisher, who said basically, 'We don't care about the team, we don't care about the league, we don't care what it turns upside down — we want all Kevin can get'."

"I've got a rule I call the $100-million rule," added outspoken guard Damon Stoudamire. "You have to be able to fill an arena on your own every night to deserve $100 million. And there are only two guys in this league capable of doing that — Michael Jordan and Shaquille O'Neal. Nobody else."

That much-debated contract eventually resulted in a ceiling being placed on NBA salaries. But Garnett's deal stands as it was negotiated. The contract will pay him a staggering $28 million in its final year (2003–4). By that time, Garnett will have made more than $131 million just for playing basketball, nearly $40 million more than what Michael Jordan earned over his 14-season career. Garnett's contract was worth between $30 and $40 million more than Glen Taylor had paid for the entire Minnesota franchise. And the really scary thing is that Garnett, at 28, will still have plenty of career left when the deal has run its course.

Rival owners called the offer to Garnett irresponsible. Many fans felt it was obscene. When the blame for the lockout was being laid, it often came to rest at the hightops of Kevin Garnett. "You really can't be mad at me because of my situation," Garnett told reporters before a charity game played during the lockout. "I had an opportunity that I took full advantage of."

It seems Garnett has indeed made the most of his opportunities. And since his jump to the NBA in 1995, other high schoolers have followed his lead. None, not even high-profile Los Angeles Laker Kobe Bryant, have had the solid success enjoyed by Garnett, however.

Would he now recommend the same jump for other high schoolers? "I've always said my decision was a decision that Kevin Maurice Garnett had to make for himself," he says. "The players accepted me with open arms and there have been nothing but positive things. Right now, my best advice is to do what you feel is right for yourself. I can't really speak on a high school star … I don't think you should make your move based on Kevin Garnett or Kobe Bryant; I think you need to evaluate your own situation."

One thing nobody can argue: The jump worked for Kevin Garnett. God-given gifts are one reason for his stunning success. But according to Flip Saunders, so is the fact Garnett is very coachable and one of the hardest workers on the floor. "The thing I've enjoyed is seeing how he really has matured as an individual," Saunders told the *Star Tribune*. "Outside people don't have any idea about the demands that are put on him. He's been in a fish bowl from the minute he left high school and was on the cover of *Sports Illustrated*. He was the pioneer for all these other people. No one had done what he did in 20 years. No one thought he would succeed as quickly as he has. There were a lot of question marks. He had a lot to live up to. Everyone (thought) he was going to fail. He put that aside and kept a strong focus."

Rob Babcock, who has happily watched Garnett mature from that initial workout in Chicago into an NBA All-Star, says each high school phenomenon must be judged separately. "I don't ever recommend kids come out of college early," he says. "You'd be crazy to recommend any high school kid to jump to the NBA. Kevin is a very special case. You won't see a case like him for another 20 years."

ESSENTIAL GARNETT

Name: Kevin Maurice Garnett
Nicknames: "KG" or "Da Kid"
Position: Forward, Minnesota Timberwolves
Born: May 19, 1976; Mauldin, SC
Height: 6'11"   **Weight:** 220 lbs.
High schools: Mauldin, South Carolina, and Farragut Academy, Chicago
College: None
Drafted: 1995, No. 5 overall by Minnesota Timberwolves

NBA

1995–96 (Timberwolves)
80 games; 43 games started; 2,293 total minutes; 28.7 minutes per game; .491 from field; .286 from three-point range; .705 from free-throw line; 501 total rebounds; 6.3 rebounds per game; 145 total assists; 1.8 assists per game; 131 blocks; 86 steals; 835 total points; 10.4 points per game.

1996–97 (Timberwolves)
77 games; 77 games started; 2,995 total minutes; 38.9 minutes per game; .499 from field; .286 from three-point range; .754 from free-throw line; 618 total rebounds; 8.0 rebounds per game; 236 total assists; 3.1 assists per game; 163 blocks; 105 steals; 1,309 total points; 17.0 points per game.

1997–98 (Timberwolves)
82 games; 82 games started; 3,222 total minutes; 39.3 minutes per game; .491 from field; .188 from three-point range; .738 from free-throw line; 786 total rebounds; 9.6 rebounds per game; 348 total assists; 4.2 assists per game; 150 blocks; 139 steals; 1,518 total points; 18.5 points per game.

1998–99 (Timberwolves)
47 games; 47 games started; 1,780 total minutes; 37.9 minutes per game; .460 from field; .286 from three-point range; .704 from free-throw line; 489 total rebounds; 10.4 rebounds per game; 202 total assists; 4.3 assists per game; 78 steals; 83 blocks; 977 total points; 20.8 points per game.

Career to date (1995–99)
286 games; 249 games started; 10,290 total minutes; 36.0 minutes per game; .486 from field; .266 from three-point range;

.730 from free-throw line; 2,394 total rebounds; 8.4 rebounds per game; 931 total assists; 3.3 assists per game; 527 blocks; 408 steals; 4,639 total points; 16.2 points per game.

Playoffs to date (1997, '98 and '99)

12 games; 12 games started; 489 total minutes; 40.8 minutes per game; .463 from field; .333 from three-point range; .771 from free-throw line; 124 total rebounds; 10.3 rebounds per game; 46 total assists; 3.8 assists per game; 23 blocks; 15 steals; 218 total points; 18.2 points per game.

NBA honours

1995–96 — NBA Rookie All-Star Game; NBA All-Rookie Second Team.

1996–97: NBA All-Star Game

1997–98: Starter in NBA All-Star Game

1998–99: All-NBA Third Team; selected to USA Basketball senior team for the 2000 Olympic Games qualifying tournament.

Sources

St. Paul *Pioneer Press*

Minneapolis *Star Tribune*

Newsweek

Inside Sports

Basketball America

Beckett Future Stars

XXL Basketball

Unlimited

CBS SportsLine

The Source

USA Today

Sports Illustrated features, June 26, 1995; Jan. 20, 1997; May 3, 1999

ESPN Pro Basketball

The Sporting News

Chicago *Tribune*

Palm Beach *Post*

New York *Times*

Miami *Herald*

Associated Press

Canadian Press

NBA.com

Official NBA Register, (regular-season) Guide and Draft Media Guide

CHAMIQUE HOLDSCLAW

Great expectations. They go with the territory when you're a No. 1 draft pick — in any professional sport, in any league, in any year. But it would be difficult to find an athlete burdened by greater expectations than Chamique Holdsclaw.

As she entered the Women's National Basketball Association (WNBA) in May of 1999, the 21-year-old Holdsclaw was being hailed as the "Michael Jordan of the women's game." Hoop hype doesn't get any bigger than that. Holdsclaw was the No. 1 overall selection of the Washington Mystics in the 1999 WNBA draft. The gifted, six-foot-two forward plays with a fluid, athletic style that has prompted some to suggest she might be capable of playing in the NBA. She was also widely portrayed as that special player who will take the WNBA, and women's basketball in general, to the next level.

As Holdsclaw entered the three-year-old professional league, even WNBA president Val Ackerman wasn't shying away from comparisons to Jordan. During the preseason, Ackerman told the media that Holdsclaw possessed the kind of star power that would help her league attract the casual fan, in much the same manner as Jordan did for the NBA. That might seem like an inordinate amount of pressure to place on one player, particularly on a soft-spoken rookie about to join a struggling

Washington franchise that had gone 3–27 the season before she arrived. But if any player is accustomed to carrying such a burden, it is Chamique Holdsclaw. The spotlight is nothing new, and neither are those expectations. They have been there since high school.

In high school, Holdsclaw helped Christ the King of Astoria to four straight New York city and state titles. From there, Chamique proceeded to college, where she powered the University of Tennessee to three consecutive National Collegiate Athletic Association (NCAA) championships. Judging by this resume, it would be easy to assume that Holdsclaw has always been a superstar and that everything has come naturally to her. But that isn't being fair to the grandmother who carefully raised her, to the coaches who shaped her career, or to the player herself who, despite being blessed with size and an abundance of natural talent, has worked hard to get where she is today.

Chamique Holdsclaw received her first basketball at the age of four. When she was just 11, with her parents freshly separated, she went to live with her grandmother in the Astoria Houses, a collection of housing projects that line New York City's East River. Chamique grew up in June Holdsclaw's six-storey building but spent much of her time on the basketball courts outside, dribbling and driving across the asphalt for as many as eight hours a day.

It was, and still is, a tough inner-city neighbourhood with its share of poverty and crime. "Yes, it's the projects," June Holdsclaw told the Knoxville *News-Sentinel* in a lengthy feature story that appeared in 1998. "But it's some good people who live here — working people." One of those good working people was June Holdsclaw herself, who raised her granddaughter with gentle discipline, stressing the importance of rules and structure while allowing Chamique to pursue her love of basketball, just as long as she wasn't skipping school, church or other responsibilities.

June Holdsclaw also sacrificed for Chamique, sometimes working an extra part-time job in addition to her position as a medical records keeper so that her granddaughter could be sent to Queen's Lutheran, a private middle school. It was there that Chamique played on her first organized basketball team, helping the school win a championship. Still, it would have been difficult to predict greatness for Chamique Holdsclaw when she went out for the girls' varsity team at Christ the King High School.

"She was actually a shy, quiet girl, with big feet and all bones," recalls Bob Mackey, an assistant basketball coach who worked nearly every day with Chamique during her four years at the parochial school. Holdsclaw wasn't an instant star in the private prep program, which under head coach Vincent Cannizzaro was already on its way to becoming a perennial powerhouse in New York state girls' basketball. In fact, Mackey remembers that he and Cannizzaro actually had a tough decision to make when Holdsclaw entered the school in the ninth grade. Did they keep her on the varsity team, where she might not get a lot of court time in her first high school season? Or did they place her on the junior varsity? Ultimately, the coaches decided that Chamique should play varsity right away. But she barely saw any court time during that freshman season, averaging about two points a game through most of the team's extensive schedule.

As Christ the King headed into the Catholic school state finals, however, the team's starting centre and its backup were both suspended for skipping practice. Holdsclaw was bumped up into the starting lineup for the championship game against rival St. Peter's of Staten

Island. Chamique responded to her first high school start in terrific fashion, scoring 14 points and grabbing 13 rebounds. It was her coming out party as a basketball prodigy. From her sophomore season on, Holdsclaw started every game for the Lady Royals, developing into a star and her school's go-to player. By her junior year, Holdsclaw and her Christ the King teammates were formidable enough to be recognized by *USA Today* as national high school champions.

During Holdsclaw's four years at the school — a period of 110 games — Christ the King would lose only four times. The Lady Royals captured four state Catholic titles and four New York Class-A state championships. Holdsclaw averaged about 18 points per game over the three seasons in which she saw substantial floor time. In her senior season, she averaged 22.5 points, 16.7 rebounds, 3.2 blocked shots and 2.4 steals per game. In fact, Holdsclaw piled up close to 2,000 points and became the first male or female to be named New York City's Player of the Year in three consecutive seasons. She was selected New York state's Class-A MVP and a *USA Today* All-American three years running. Included in the national player-of-the-year honours she captured were the Naismith Award from the Atlanta Tip-Off Club, the Columbus, Ohio Touchdown Club award and the Rawlings/Women's Basketball Coaches Association (WBCA) award.

By the time she left Christ the King, Holdsclaw had gone from shy, timid freshman to the finest high school prospect in the country. She had blossomed into an athletic, versatile player who was capable of outstanding play as a wing, forward or centre. She had improved tremendously during her four seasons at the Astoria school. Part of that improvement was due to a natural maturation process, but much of it was due to hard work as Chamique and her coaches spent hours in the gym concentrating on individual skills. Her game thrived on the competitive playgrounds of Queens. "She was the best girls' high school player I've seen," Bob Mackey says now. "I've seen better post players, better guards, better forwards, but Chamique brings everything to the table. She has the elements to do whatever she wants."

By her junior year in high school, Holdsclaw also had all the elements to be the top college recruit in the U.S. Hundreds of schools were interested in an athletic, six-foot-one player who could score, rebound, jump, pass and handle the ball. But Chamique and her grandmother quickly narrowed the field to a handful of universities and worked from there. Both grandmother and granddaughter were impressed by the home visit from Tennessee coach Pat Summitt and her top assistant and chief recruiter Mickie DeMoss. And after the Holdsclaws made their own recruiting visit to the Tennessee campus in Knoxville, the choice was made.

In Tennessee, Holdsclaw was going to a dominant collegiate program, much like the high school system she was leaving at Christ the King. She was also going to the South, an area her grandmother, an Alabama native, felt would provide a positive environment. June Holdsclaw also appreciated the fact that the Lady Vols program demanded discipline from its players and that coach Summitt had stressed that her granddaughter would be expected to earn her playing time. "It kind of just all fit together," Mickie DeMoss says now.

The Tennessee Lady Volunteers have long been one of the premier programs in the U.S. women's college game. They had won three national titles before Chamique Holdsclaw arrived on campus and have turned out an array of polished players during the quarter century Summitt has served as the school's head coach. Tennessee has the most successful women's basketball program of all-time in the U.S. and, under Summitt, the team has amassed a record of 695 wins against 146 defeats. The Lady Vols are immensely popular in Knoxville, drawing huge crowds to the Thompson-Boling Arena on a regular basis. But Chamique Holdsclaw's star power was enough to change even the grand face of Tennessee basketball. By her senior year, she was not able to venture to the local mall without being inundated by autograph seekers. And in her final season at Tennessee, the Lady Vols averaged a national-record 16,565 fans per game.

"I don't think any of us could have ever imagined the impact she'd have, not only on our program, but on the women's game in general," says DeMoss, who has coached 14 seasons at Tennessee and recently was rated as the top women's assistant in the NCAA by a poll of head coaches. "We knew Chamique was a good athlete when she came out of high school, but we didn't know if she would step up her game when she got here," DeMoss adds. "From day one, she stepped up."

Indeed, it would be difficult to imagine one player having a bigger impact on the college basketball scene. During her first three seasons in Knoxville, Chamique Holdsclaw led the Lady Vols to three straight NCAA titles. During her final two years, she was a consensus national player of the year. Holdsclaw finished her career in Knoxville as the all-time leading rebounder (1,295) and scorer (3,025) — men's or women's — in Tennessee hoops history. Over her four years as a Lady Vol, she averaged 20.4 points, 8.8 rebounds and 2.3 assists. She was only the fourth player ever to become a four-time Kodak All-American and the first to earn three Associated Press first-team honours. As a senior, she won the prestigious James E. Sullivan Award, given to the most outstanding amateur athlete in the entire U.S. In the 69-year history of the award, it was the first time a women's basketball player had been honoured. Holdsclaw even had a street named after her on the Tennessee campus.

"Basketball has always been prominent at Tennessee, but she put us at a different level," Mickie DeMoss says now. "She's made an impact in recruiting. Everybody wants to be the next Chamique." DeMoss does recall, however, that it wasn't all smooth sailing for Holdsclaw during her college days. "There were a couple of times during her freshman and sophomore years when Chamique had some academic troubles and she was getting pressure from Pat and (academic people)," DeMoss says. "She was struggling in class and she came to me once and said: 'I'm leaving. I'm calling my grandmother and she's coming to get me.' I just said: 'OK Chamique, if that's what you want, I'll call your grandmother.' She just looked at me like: 'Are you crazy?' "

Fortunately for everybody involved, Chamique wasn't going anywhere. She would remain at Knoxville for the four-year duration, graduating in May 1999 with a degree in Political Science. On the court, meanwhile, she and the rest of the talented Lady Vols majored in victories. During Holdsclaw's college career, Tennessee lost just 17 of 148 games. The highlight was her junior season, when the Lady Vols went a perfect 39–0, piling up the most victories ever recorded by a college basketball team in a single campaign. In NCAA Tournament play during Holdsclaw's career, the Lady Vols went an incredible 21–1. Sadly, their only post-season loss came in Holdsclaw's final game as a collegian.

It was a strange way for perhaps the finest player in NCAA history to bow out. In the East Regional final at the Greensboro Coliseum, Holdsclaw suffered through a rare off-day as her powerful team fell to Duke 69–63 in a huge upset. Holdsclaw went just 2-for-18 from the field for eight points and fouled out with 25.4 seconds remaining to a standing ovation from the largely pro-Tennessee crowd. After averaging better than 29 points per game in her three previous 1999 tournament appearances, this was a tough way to say goodbye. Tougher still, though, was the fact the Lady Vols had come up short in their quest to win an unprecedented four straight national titles. "Chamique took (the loss) hard," DeMoss says. "She felt like she let the team down and let us down. It was a blow for her and (four-year point guard) Kellie Jolly, because they were so close to doing something that will probably never be done. But she bounced back and set her sights on the WNBA."

Meanwhile, the WNBA was setting its sights on Chamique. As the league entered its third season, it was moving out of the novelty stage and not so subtly looking to Holdsclaw to bring more fans on board. With her height and the ability to create her own shots, Holdsclaw generated a buzz whenever she stepped on the floor. Quite simply, she did things other female players couldn't. This was a player who could handle the ball, shoot from the outside, post-up her defender, rebound and pass. And her defence — her weak suit coming into Tennessee — had improved dramatically during her time at Knoxville. Moreover, Holdsclaw was already a veteran on the powerful U.S. national team and, despite being the squad's lone collegian, had led the U.S. in both scoring and rebounding at the 1997 world championship qualifying tournament in Brazil.

"She does so many things exceptionally well," DeMoss said after Holdsclaw's departure from college. "She's very difficult to guard. She can take you off the dribble, shoot off the pass, post you up. There are not many female players who are that athletic and that highly skilled. But I think the thing that really separates her is that she finishes. She finishes those moves that other female players are just learning." It is this special talent, this smooth flash, that made Chamique Holdsclaw the most sought-after player in the 1999 WNBA draft — a lofty status when you consider that this particular draft contained the cream of the crop from the disbanded American Basketball League (ABL), the former rival of the WNBA. Thirty-five of the 50 players selected in the draft would be former ABL stars, a list that included a handful of U.S. Olympians and some of the top basketball talent in the world. Chamique was the only college player selected in the first round, but there was never much doubt about her place in the draft.

There was, however, considerable talk about where Holdsclaw would end up playing her first professional season. Although the Washington Mystics, coming off a dismal 3–27 season, owned the No. 1 pick, there was speculation that the league would step in and somehow orchestrate Chamique Holdsclaw's placement with her hometown New York Liberty. It was thought that the combination of the pre-eminent young superstar with the country's most important market would be a shrewd marketing move. But to the WNBA's credit, it conducted itself professionally, leaving the picks up to the teams themselves and playing the draft by the book.

"A lot of people wanted me to play in New York," Holdsclaw told the New York *Times*. "I'm kind of glad I didn't. I don't know if I could have handled the pressure and the fans." Going to the Mystics was an appealing situation to Holdsclaw for a couple of reasons: The team had the WNBA's most loyal fans and Washington's new head coach Nancy Darsch was a former Tennessee assistant who was highly recommended by Pat Summitt.

As for the Mystics, there wasn't much question —
Chamique was their pick. Despite the team's terrible
record the previous season, 15,910 fans a game had
turned out to watch the Washington franchise. Now,
with Chamique Holdsclaw arriving to play in the MCI
Center, the excitement was building well before the first
tip-off. "She is a tremendous basketball player and she
is going to be loved, not only by this city, but by every
WNBA city that we travel to," Nancy Darsch told the
Baltimore *Sun* after the team made the pick official.
"Over time she will become a dominant player in this
league. If that happens next month, that's all the better.
But it will happen eventually. It will happen over time."

When it came to hype, time didn't seem necessary.
Many were ready to instantly anoint Holdsclaw as the
greatest women's player ever. It was widely estimated that,
including endorsements, Holdsclaw had instantly become the WNBA's highest paid player, making more
than the $250,000 U.S. earned by incumbent stars such
as Sheryl Swoopes, Lisa Leslie and Rebecca Lobo. Was
she the league's best player? "There are lot of better shoot-
ers and lot of better defenders," Holdsclaw told the
Washington *Post* on draft day, "(but) the way I play is
unique. I know there aren't many females who play the
game the way I do."

"The fact that she was the first player chosen out of
an incredible group of players speaks volumes about her,"
WNBA president Val Ackerman told the media. "She's
the player of the present and the player of the future for
our league." The proof wasn't long in arriving. For her
professional debut, a sellout crowd of 20,674 fans packed
the MCI Center to watch Holdsclaw score 18 points
and add six rebounds in an 83–73 loss to the Charlotte
Sting. Then, in her celebrated return to New York,
Chamique piled up 20 points and nine rebounds to help

the Mystics shake off an 0–2 start and post their first win of the season, an 83–61 decision over the Liberty at Madison Square Garden.

Holdsclaw's place amongst the game's all-time best players remains to be determined. One thing is certain, though: She has the highest profile in the WNBA. And with that profile comes time-consuming responsibilities. Ever since the draft, Holdsclaw has been swamped with interview requests and demands on her time. She barely had a chance to finish school at Tennessee, graduate and serve as a bridesmaid for former Lady Vols teammate Kellie Jolly's wedding before being thrown headfirst into the pro game and expected to dominate. For most players, that pressure would be new and potentially intimidating. But for Holdsclaw it is old hat. "I've been in the spotlight ever since high school so it's not something that's new to me," she told the Boston *Globe*. "Everyone says, 'Chamique does an exceptional job at handling it' but that's 'cause I'm kind of used to it."

As her former high school assistant coach Bob Mackey says: "She got used to being in the spotlight at Christ the King." And that continued at Tennessee, where Holdsclaw accommodated more than 700 interview and picture requests during her senior season, prompting Lady Vols staff to limit such engagements to four per day. If any player has been prepared to handle the onslaught of attention and deflect the overload of hype, it is Holdsclaw. "She still has humility. I hope she can maintain that," says Mickie DeMoss.

"She handles it great," Mystics teammate Nikki McCray told the Associated Press. "She comes to practice, works hard, stays focused. Goes home, sits on the couch, goes to the movies and chills out with her friends. She's done a great job of handling everything."

And as for the comparisons with Jordan — well,

they are only fuelled by the fact Chamique wears No. 23, just like Mike. She is certainly a Jordan fan, but tells people she actually wears the number because of the 23rd Psalm which includes the verse: "The Lord is my shepherd, I shall not want." There are some on-court similarities, however, between the two No. 23s. "She sees the floor very well. She plays with a smoothness and an efficiency," Mystics coach Nancy Darsch told the Associated Press. "She never seems to be in a panic or in a hurry. She's in her own tempo, and it's a productive tempo. She (also) has very good natural ability with her size. She's been well coached, she's been a good student of the game, and when she works hard at it, I think she is in another class. She's one of the few women players that — as some of the NBA scouts like to say — can get her own shot. She can get up over people, and I think she and (Sheryl) Swoopes probably do that better than anybody I've ever seen."

One thing to remember when trying to pinpoint Holdsclaw's place among the game's greats is that she is still young. Her coaches will tell you that Chamique Holdsclaw is a player who works hard at getting better. Asked what separates Holdsclaw from other gifted athletes, Bob Mackey is quick to respond. "That's an easy one," he says. "Chamique has that work ethic that today a lot of players don't have. She works hard at what she does. She could do anything and be successful at it. It all looks very smooth on the basketball court and very easy, but she's worked at it."

Holdsclaw made it look easy during her first pro season, averaging 16.9 points, 7.9 rebounds and 2.4 assists to wrap up WNBA Rookie of the Year and All-Star honours and help the Mystics improve to 12-20. "You come in, you're labelled this hotshot, this great player," Holdsclaw told the Associated Press. "I think a lot of players wouldn't be able to handle all the attention … I think I have my teammates' respect because I'm a team player first. I know what I can do, and I'm going to do it when it's needed. Just play within the team concept and your individual talent will shine."

PURE CHAMIQUE

Name: Chamique Shaunta Holdsclaw
Nicknames: "Mique" or "Meek"
Position: Forward, Washington Mystics
Born: August 9, 1977; Flushing, NY
Height: 6'2"   **Weight:** 167 lbs.
High school: Christ the King, Astoria, NY
College: University of Tennessee, Knoxville, TN
Drafted: 1999, No. 1 overall by Washington Mystics

COLLEGE

As a freshman (1995-96)
36 games; .467 from field; .233 from three-point range; .713 from free-throw line; 326 total rebounds; 9.1 rebounds per game; 75 total assists; 2.1 assists per game; 583 total points; 16.2 points per game.

As a sophomore (1996-97)
39 games; .495 from field; .340 from three-point range; .667 from free-throw line; 367 total rebounds; 9.4 rebounds per game; 114 total assists; 2.9 assists per game; 803 total points; 20.6 points per game.

As a junior (1997-98)
39 games; .546 from field; .220 from three-point range; .765 from free-throw line; 915 total points; 23.5 points per game; 328 total rebounds; 8.4 rebounds per game; 117 total assists; 3.0 assists per game; 915 total points; 23.5 points per game.

As a senior (1998-99)
34 games; .519 from field; .143 from three-point range; .707 from free-throw line; 274 total rebounds; 8.1 rebounds per game; 80 total assists; 2.35 assists per game; 724 total points; 21.3 points per game.

College career (1995-99)

148 games; .510 from field; .254 from three-point range; .715 from free-throw line; 1,295 total rebounds; 8.8 rebounds per game; 336 total assists; 2.27 assists per game; 3025 total points; 20.4 points per game.

College honours

1995-96 — Final Four All-Tournament team; East Regional All-Tournament team; Kodak All-American; Associated Press (AP) Third Team All-American; United Press International Third Team All-American; *College Sports* magazine Second Team All-American; U.S. Basketball Writers Association (USBWA) All-American; USBWA Rookie of the Year; All-Southeastern Conference (SEC) First Team.

1996-97 — Honda Award for Basketball; Final Four Outstanding Player and All-Tournament team; Midwest Regional Outstanding Player and All-Tournament team; Women's Sports Player of the Year (*Sports Illustrated*); Columbus (Ohio) Touchdown Club Player of the Year; Naismith Award finalist; ESPY Women's Basketball Player of the Year finalist; Kodak All-American; AP First Team All-American; Naismith First Team All-American; *The Sporting News* First Team All-American; USBWA First Team All-American; unanimous All-SEC First Team; All-SEC Tournament team; Women's NIT All-Tournament team.

1997-98 — Honda-Broderick Cup for NCAA Outstanding Female Athlete of the Year; SEC Female Athlete of the Year; Naismith Player of the Year; AP Player of the Year; Rawlings/Women's Basketball Coaches Association (WBCA) Player of the Year; *The Sporting News* Player of the Year; USBWA Player of the Year; *Women's Basketball Journal* Player of the Year; Frontier/State Farm Player of the Year; Columbus (Ohio) Touchdown Club Player of the Year; Final Four Outstanding Player and All-Tournament team; Mideast Regional Outstanding Player and All-Tournament team; Kodak All-American; AP First Team All-American; Naismith First Team All-American; *The Sporting News* First Team All-American; USBWA First Team All-American; SEC Player of the Year and All-SEC First Team; SEC Tournament MVP and All-Tournament team; ESPY Award for Women's Basketball Player of the Year; AAU James E. Sullivan Memorial Award finalist; USA Basketball Player of the Year.

1998-99 — Kodak 25th Anniversary All-American team;

Women's Basketball Journal, Sports Illustrated and *The Sporting News* National Women's Player of the Year; Naismith Player of the Year; East Regional All-Tournament team; AP Player of the Year: WBCA Player of the Year; Naismith Player of the Year; James E. Sullivan Award winner; Kodak All-American; AP All-American; WBCA All-American; SEC Female Athlete of the Year; ESPY Award (female athlete of the year); ESPY Award (women's basketball player of the year); SEC Tournament MVP.

College records

Southeastern Conference's all-time leading scorer; third on all-time NCAA women's career scoring list; No. 1 scorer and rebounder in history of University of Tennessee basketball; NCAA Tournament career leader in points (479) and rebounds (200).

WNBA

1998–99 (Washington Mystics)

31 games; 34.2 minutes per game; .437 from field; .172 from three-point range; .773 from free-throw line; 7.9 rebounds per game; 2.4 assists per game; 37 steals; 27 blocks; 525 total points; 16.9 points per game.

WNBA honours

All-WNBA second team; selected to All-Star game; WNBA Rookie of the Year.

Sources

Knoxville *News-Sentinel* feature, Aug. 30, 1998
Sports Illustrated feature, April 6, 1998
New York *Times*
Baltimore *Sun*
Washington *Post*
Boston *Globe*
Associated Press
University of Tennessee Lady Volunteers website
WNBA.com
Official WNBA Guide and Register

ALLEN IVERSON

In so many ways, he was just like the other athletes profiled in this book. He was the high school superstar, the wondrously gifted leader capable of arriving at a big-time college and making an immediate impact on its basketball program. With one exception. None of the other athletes began a college career after serving a nearly four-month stint on a state prison farm. And none had to endure the special scrutiny focused on Allen Iverson when he arrived at Georgetown University as a freshman point guard in the Fall of 1994.

Iverson entered the Washington, D.C., school under a cloud of controversy. Just 19 months earlier, he had been involved in an ugly bowling-alley brawl in his hometown of Hampton, Virginia. According to witnesses, the fight was racially charged. When the smoke cleared, two people were unconscious, including a female college student who had been cut near her left eye with a chair. It took six stitches to repair the physical damage. And four alleged participants — all black — had been arrested. Among them was Allen Iverson.

Iverson wasn't just any Hampton high schooler. He was a two-sport superstar at Bethel High: an explosive quarterback and defensive safety for the varsity football team; and the all-everything point guard who averaged 31.6 points per game as a junior. In fact, in 1992-93

Iverson was Virginia's player of the year in football *and* basketball, and led Bethel to state championships in both sports. Through his exploits, Iverson had gained notoriety in his hometown and across the state. In September of 1993, many felt he was being persecuted because of that notoriety. By the time the case had proceeded through the justice system, Iverson had been convicted of three counts of "maiming by mob." Instead of probation or similar light punishment, he had been sentenced to a total of 15 years in prison, with 10 years suspended. Bail was denied while Iverson and two others appealed.

These harsh sentences touched off a storm of protests from those who believed that the severity of the punishment was racially weighted and that Iverson had been targeted because he was a high-profile black athlete. "It's strange enough that the police waded through a huge mob of fighting people and came out with only blacks, and the one black that everybody knew," National Association for the Advancement of Colored People (NAACP) crisis coordinator Golden Frinks told *Sports Illustrated.* "But people thought they'd get a slap on the wrist and that would be the end of it." In reality, it was only the beginning of a personal nightmare for Allen Iverson. He went on to serve nearly four months at the Newport News City Farm, a minimum-security work camp. This stretch of time included holidays away from family and friends — away from life as the teenager had known it. And, of course, away from high-school basketball. After four months, Virginia governor Douglas Wilder granted him conditional clemency. He was allowed to return home on the condition he complete his high-school diploma, undergo counselling, maintain a nightly curfew and not participate in any prep sports.

Prior to his incarceration, Allen Iverson had been a

sought-after college basketball prospect. He had been named *Parade Magazine's* top-rated U.S. high schooler. He was a highly athletic, utterly fearless scoring machine — a player college coaches had long since noted on their recruiting radar. As it turned out, however, the "recruitment" process for Iverson would be unique. Despite his legal problems and the fact he hadn't played a senior season in high school, some programs remained interested in offering him a scholarship. But thanks largely to his mother, Iverson ended up at a school that hadn't actively recruited him.

While her son was still in prison, Ann Iverson paid a visit to highly respected Georgetown University coach John Thompson. Now a Basketball Hall of Famer, Thompson had carved out a reputation as both a disciplinarian and a molder of young men, not simply young basketball players. Ann Iverson tearfully asked Thompson to give her son a second chance, a new start in both life and basketball. The coach agreed. "Regardless of what's happened in the past, Allen is a bright young man who deserves a chance to pursue a college education," Thompson told *Sports Illustrated* at the time. "He will have to follow the same rules and accomplish the same things in the classroom as anyone else in this program."

Georgetown's current head coach Craig Esherick was a longtime assistant to Thompson when Iverson entered the Hoyas program in the Fall of 1994. He remembers a tough, talented youngster in a hurry to make up for lost time. "Here was a kid who did not play organized basketball for one whole year — something he loves to do, something that defines him as a person," Esherick says now. "Then all of a sudden, he receives a chance to play at Georgetown. He attempted to get back that year as quickly as he could." As a result, the talented freshman had a tendency to rush things. Or as CBS commentator Billy Packer pointed out, it seemed as though Iverson was trying to make All-American on the very first possession of the very first game. "He was in a hurry to prove himself," Esherick agrees. "He had to relax, let the game come to him."

Other than that, the Georgetown coach says Iverson dealt extremely well with a difficult situation. He played on, even when some opposing fans dressed up as convicts and others carried signs that were in questionable taste. "He handled it all very well," Esherick says. "There certainly were many things that were said that I considered very unfair. But Allen was also 19, 20 years old, and some of it *did* bother him." Not that he showed it on the court, however. Iverson would average 20.4 points, 4.5 assists and 3.3 rebounds per game for the 21–10 Hoyas during his sparkling freshman National Collegiate Athletic Association (NCAA) season. He was named Rookie of the Year in the highly regarded Big East Conference. He was also a second-team All-Big East selection and he was chosen the conference's Defensive Player of the Year after posting a Georgetown-freshman record of 89 steals.

But more than mere numbers electrified those who congregated at Georgetown's games that season. Iverson entered the school barely six-feet-tall and with deceptively skinny legs that one longtime Hoyas observer described as "bird stems." But those legs could make the Virginia youngster fly like few other players in college basketball. His all-out hustle at both ends of the floor made him a crowd favourite. Georgetown fans fell in love with Iverson's fearless forays into the paint, his lightning crossover dribble that froze defenders, his quickness and raw speed that helped him blow past opponents and his penchant for soaring before scoring in dramatic fashion. Even summer league games became an event with Iverson wearing the school uniform.

While Iverson flourished on the court at Georgetown, John Thompson's rigid program also seemed to be good for him. The coach had a long-established rule that freshmen weren't to be the subject of media interviews during their entire first semester at the school. Thompson's logic was that freshman wouldn't be able to comment knowledgeably on school or NCAA basketball until they had experienced some of both. The rule was in place for everyone, but it particularly helped Iverson, who might have found himself the focus of much more unwanted attention had he attended another school. Meanwhile, it seemed clear that Thompson's authoritarian style was also paying dividends for Iverson's development, both as a person and a player. "No question about it, John Thompson played a huge role in his life," Craig Esherick says.

Although he was initially somewhat shielded from the spotlight off the floor, it was difficult not to notice the freshman when he hit the hardwood. During the 1994–95 season, Iverson became only the second Georgetown player to score 30 or more points in consecutive games. He tallied 31 points against Miami in the Big East tournament and he notched 24 more in a third-round NCAA Tournament loss to North Carolina. More important to the coaches, however, was the fact Allen Iverson proved to be an extremely smart kid and a very coachable player who was co-operative and easy to get along with, traits that might have surprised those who had been quick to paint him as "troubled" following his stint in prison. "He's always been a very pleasant kid to be around," Esherick says. "All the guys on the team loved him."

Something else that struck both the coaching staff

and fans was Iverson's speed and endurance. Esherick had never seen a player as well-conditioned or as fast. And head coach John Thompson absolutely loved his effort even if at times the freshman's play was erratic. "I tell the kids, if everybody on the floor plays as hard as he does, then I'll let you make some bad judgments, too," Thompson would later tell the Washington *Post*. It was obvious the rookie possessed a ton of self-confidence. And he was also one of the most competitive players who had ever worn the colours of Georgetown, a college with an illustrious basketball program that had already produced future NBA impact players Patrick Ewing and Alonzo Mourning. "I had watched him since he was a tenth grader," Esherick recalls. "He had been on an Amateur Athletic Union (AAU) team that had won several tournaments. Every coach in the country was familiar with his game. But Allen still amazed me every day in practice with something that he did. He never lost a sprint the whole time that he was here ... He is as competitive as anyone we've ever had here."

Any concerns about Iverson's size — he is barely six feet and not more than 165 pounds — were short-lived. He quickly showed that he didn't back down from anybody, in games or on the practice floor. "The harder he got knocked down, the quicker he would get up," Esherick says. "I think he gets that from football. He didn't want to be perceived as frail or weak. He took some shots in practice from guys where I didn't think he would get up. But he would just bounce up off the floor."

As impressed as the Georgetown staff had been with Iverson's rookie year, he would improve substantially before his sophomore season. In the summer of 1995, Iverson was named to the U.S. team for the World University Games in Japan. There he was instrumental in steering the undefeated Americans to the gold medal, leading the star-studded team in scoring, assists and steals.

Happily for Iverson, his legal troubles ended and his name was cleared between his first and second years at Georgetown. His convictions from the bowling alley incident were overturned in the summer of 1995 when the Virginia Court of Appeals determined that there was reasonable doubt about his involvement. Allen Iverson had weathered a stormy period in his life that might have destroyed other young men. "I don't know if, as a child, I would have been able to handle what he's handled," John Thompson told the Washington *Post*. "Throughout his whole ordeal, I never saw the man cry." As for Iverson himself, he preferred to look ahead and stick to basketball, at least when it came to his public comments. "It's a great feeling to have all that behind me," he told the Associated Press (AP).

By the time his second college campaign rolled around, Iverson was ready to take his performance up another notch. "Compared to last year, I feel a lot more comfortable," he told the New York *Daily News* before the 1995–96 season began. "I have a whole year under my belt and that experience alone should help." It certainly seemed to. Not only did Iverson bump up his scoring average by more than 4.5 points to an even 25 per game, he also improved his field-goal percentage by nearly 10 percent to a healthy .480. As well, the super sophomore raised his three-point accuracy (from .232 to .366), his assists (4.5 to 4.7) and his rebounds (3.3 to 3.8). He also established a Georgetown single-season record for steals (124), quite an accomplishment in a program with the nickname "Defence U."

"The thing I remember the most is just the improvement that Allen made between his freshman and sophomore years," recalls Craig Esherick. "The growth he had in that time was phenomenal in terms of him understanding the game, taking the good shots as opposed to the bad shots. We became a better team because of it." Indeed, Iverson's growth helped power the Hoyas all the way to the 1996 NCAA Tournament East Regional championship game, where they fell to UMass despite their star guard's 24-point performance. For the tournament, Iverson averaged an eye-opening 27.8 points per game. During the first two games of that NCAA Tournament, Iverson was also able to make a triumphant return to his home state. The Hoyas opened their regional in Richmond, just an hour away from Iverson's home in Hampton. And among the friends and supporters in the crowd was former Virginia governor Douglas Wilder, the man whose clemency ruling had made it possible for Iverson to resume his basketball career and, indeed, his life. "You can't imagine how good it makes you feel when you catch a kid who could have easily slipped off the slope," Wilder told reporters at that game.

Iverson's accomplishments on the court during his sophomore campaign did not go unrewarded. For the second straight season, he was named Big East Defensive Player of the Year and he was also a unanimous All-Big East First Team selection. Despite leading the conference in scoring and being the league's top defender, Iverson was not selected Big East Player of the Year, however. That award went to Connecticut's junior shooting guard Ray Allen. Nevertheless, Iverson was anointed a First-Team All-American by both the Associated Press and *The Sporting News*. He had also become a near-consensus No. 1 pick in the 1996 NBA draft — if, as it was widely speculated, he decided to leave college early.

Pro scouts drooled over Iverson's quickness, his ability to break down defences off the dribble and his leaping ability. They also loved his effort at both ends of the floor, his athleticism and his competitiveness. Nearly everyone believed Iverson's game would be even better suited to the NBA, a league without the zone defences found in college and in which the ability to create shots is at a premium. Pound for pound and inch for inch, Iverson was widely considered to be the best college basketball had to offer in this draft. Whether Allen Iverson would stay or go pro was a question that college basketball fans, and Georgetown followers in particular, were loudly posing as the 1995–96 season concluded. In fact, during one Saturday matinee against Villanova in early March, while Iverson was exploding for a brilliant 37 points, fans began to plead, in unison: "Two more years! Two more years!"

On May 1, he ended the speculation by calling a press conference to make it official: Allen Iverson was declaring himself eligible for the draft. In doing so, he became the first player in John Thompson's 24-year tenure at the D.C. school to leave early for the NBA.

"After carefully weighing my options with coach Thompson and my family, I've decided to enter the NBA draft," Iverson told reporters during the news conference at McDonough Arena, where he was flanked by Thompson. "I definitely plan to further my education, but my family needs to be addressed right now." That family included his one-year-old daughter, Tiaura, as well as his younger sister who had been experiencing frightening seizures and required expensive medical attention. By going pro, Iverson could help his family immediately. If, as predicted, he went No. 1 overall, he would sign a three-year deal for about $3 million U.S. per season, more than enough to take care of all of his family's wants and needs for years. "All of those things went into Allen's decision," Esherick explains.

By the time the NBA Draft rolled around at East Rutherford, New Jersey, there was little doubt as to what the Philadelphia 76ers would do with their No. 1 overall pick. Allen Iverson was the first player called to the podium by NBA commissioner David Stern. Iverson was about to begin what would be an interesting first three seasons in the NBA.

As a rookie, Iverson made a couple of indelible impressions. The first was of an undeniable talent, an athletic backcourt force to be reckoned with. He burst onto the scene by averaging 23.5 points, 7.5 assists and 4.1 rebounds per game and captured NBA Rookie of the Year honours despite playing on a team that struggled to a 22–60 record. In one memorable game, he left the legendary Michael Jordan grasping at air after beating him with his patented crossover dribble.

The second impression Iverson made wasn't so positive. He quickly became stereotyped as a poster boy for everything that was wrong with young players in the league. In many peoples' eyes, Iverson was a brash, cocky youngster who didn't show nearly enough respect for the veterans or the protocol of the NBA. Charles Barkley derisively referred to him as the "playground rookie of the year." Iverson was booed during the Rookie All-Star Game at Cleveland's Gund Arena after comments he made about Jordan and other veterans were misconstrued. Near the end of the season, Iverson and the 76ers were also criticized for what was widely seen as a blatant attempt to lock up the Rookie of the Year vote by helping Iverson to score 40 or more points in five straight games and break Wilt Chamberlain's freshman scoring record. During that same rookie season, the league tried to curb his crossover move. And an NBA edict curtailing shorts that were overly baggy seemed to be aimed at the 76ers guard.

Those negative feelings were only compounded by off-the-court news about Iverson. In August of 1997, a few months after his rookie campaign was completed, Iverson was a passenger in a car that was stopped for speeding on an interstate highway near Richmond, Virginia. A .45-calibre pistol and a small amount of marijuana were found during a police search. Later that month, Iverson pleaded no contest to carrying a concealed weapon and was placed on three years' probation. The marijuana charges were dropped. Iverson's name hit the news again in July of 1998, when two men driving a car owned by the player were arrested in Norfolk, Virginia, after allegedly completing a drug deal.

During his second year with the 76ers, a season in which his scoring (22.0) and assist (6.2) averages both dipped, Iverson skipped a practice and was suspended for a game. This, along with the off-court news he had been making, resulted in Iverson being painted as an incorrigible bad-boy by the mainstream media. He was being criticized for not choosing his friends correctly, for travelling with a "posse." Iverson protested. "I don't care about other peoples' friends," he told the Vancouver *Province*, "so why should anybody care about mine?"

Part of the problem with the way Iverson and many other young, black athletes are sometimes portrayed is that their stories are often relayed by white, middle-aged, male sportswriters, most of whom come from strikingly different backgrounds than Allen Iverson. Iverson wears several tattoos, one of which contains the telling phrase: "Only the strong survive." According to an Associated Press report, in one summer alone as he grew up, eight of his friends were killed. It is difficult for the average sportswriter to conceive of this when passing judgment on Iverson's actions or words. Sometimes Iverson is also a convenient target. When the issue of what's wrong with the young stars of the NBA is raised, his name is automatically trotted out. There have also been criticisms of Iverson's game. Despite the fact that his shooting percentage actually climbed by nearly five percent during his second NBA season, his assists dropped by 1.3 per game. Critics were quick to jump on him for being a "selfish" player and, coupled with the off-court controversy, Iverson's bad-boy image grew.

"Allen had his maturation process in the the NBA," Georgetown coach Craig Esherick says. "That process was more public than it would have been in college. In college it's more sheltered. In the pros, you're not protected at all. In the pros you perform in a goldfish bowl." Still, as freelance journalist Larry Platt pointed out so effectively in a revealing 1999 *Hoop Magazine* article, that goldfish bowl has rarely allowed people to catch a full glimpse of Allen Iverson. It hasn't revealed the many sick children the 76ers star has quietly visited in hospitals. It hasn't told the story of The Crossover Foundation, Iverson's charitable arm that has helped save the Boys & Girls Club in his hometown from closing its doors permanently. It hasn't shown Iverson as an accomplished artist — he pens caricatures and hopes to concentrate full-time on his drawing when his basketball career is over — and it hasn't shown Iverson the young father, who is now raising a son, Allen II (Deuce), as well as his daughter, Tiaura.

Iverson clearly doesn't court the media spotlight, especially on those many occasions when he is asked to comfort a sick child. "That's not why I do it," he told Platt. "It's not fair to see a sick kid and he's gotta have all these cameras around him, like I'm visiting him to make me look good to the media. I'm just there to make the kid feel good."

"People make mistakes," Iverson added in the same

thoughtful article. "But as long as I can look Deuce, Tiaura and my family in their eyes and know they know I'm not a bad guy, that's what really matters to me." Iverson also seems rather resigned to the fact that he will be unfairly portrayed and criticized by those who don't take the time to understand him. He once said that "today's newspaper is tomorrow's toilet paper," showing his disdain for many of the journalists who cover his sport. During a 1999 television interview, he said that he had already determined what he wants on his tombstone. The inscription of choice? "Misunderstood."

"He's a decent kid," Larry Brown, his Philadelphia coach, told Canadian Press. "We all make mistakes. I don't think any mistakes he makes are malicious. If you ask the guys on his team, they all like him and have lots of respect for him." Iverson says his only pressing basketball goal is to go deep into the playoffs and to help the 76ers compete for an NBA title. And Brown has said more than once that Iverson is not a selfish player. Nevertheless, that image still persists. "I'm used to the criticism," Iverson told Canadian Press during the 1999 season. "I could have the greatest season, win a championship, do it all and I'm still going to be criticized. I know people are going to take shots at me all through my career and they're going to do that when I'm finished. I always say there's a million people out there that love you and a million that are going to hate you. Concentrate on the ones that love you."

Plenty of Philadelphians fell in love with Allen Iverson during his first two years in the NBA. But he absolutely captivated the City of Brotherly Love in his third year, after coach Larry Brown moved him from point guard to shooting guard. During the lockout-shortened 1999 season, the six-foot Iverson became the shortest player in NBA history to win the league scoring title, averaging 26.8 points per game to edge one of the game's biggest players, seven-foot-one, 315-pound Shaquille O'Neal, who averaged 26.3 points. Prior to Iverson, the shortest league scoring champion had been six-foot-one Boston Celtics guard Nate "Tiny" Archibald in the 1972–73 season.

Iverson wasn't simply a scorer during his spectacular third season, either. His ability to draw defensive double-teams meant easier rebounding and scoring opportunities for many of his teammates. And along with his points, he posted 4.6 assists, 4.9 rebounds and 2.29 steals per game. "Good players make other players better," Larry Brown told the New York *Times*. "I didn't know when I first got here if that was the case with Allen ... But from the second half of last season and this year, he's doing what great players do: Making other players better." Most importantly for Philly basketball fans, he was also making his team better. In his third season, Allen Iverson led the Sixers to their first playoff berth in eight long years.

Iverson's exploits earned him First Team All-NBA honours for the first time in his career. Many felt, however, that he was shortchanged after he finished fourth in the balloting for the league MVP award behind winner Karl Malone, Alonzo Mourning and Tim Duncan. But Iverson, showing a maturity that comes with age, wasn't about to dwell on the slight. In fact, during a press conference to announce his All-NBA selection, Iverson was gracious, giving credit to his 76ers teammates for helping him achieve the honour. "It does feel good," he said, "to know that people will recognize me for something positive. And it makes me feel like I've come a long way to get something accomplished like this. I felt for me to win that (MVP) award, I had to do more than I did this year. It really was just an honour for me to be mentioned as one of the top players in the league."

And just what does he have to accomplish to become an MVP? "His shot selection has got to get better," Larry Brown told the Associated Press. "He has got to get a more consistent outside shot, and he has got to be a better defender. If he works on those areas of the game, the guy has a chance to be considered for MVP. Michael, Magic, Isiah Thomas, they all did it."

Iverson showed just how far he has already come by powering the surprising 76ers into the second round of the 1999 playoffs. During a first-round win over the Orlando Magic, he was clearly the difference, scoring 30 or more points in three of the four games. His playoff peak came in front of a delirious hometown crowd in Game 3, when he pumped in 33 points, added five assists, committed just two turnovers and posted 10 steals, an NBA single-game playoff record. As the home team whipped its fans into a frenzy, Ann Iverson could be spotted on the NBC cameras, dressed in her 76ers jersey and holding a blue banner, reading: "That's My Boy, No. 3, Allen Iverson." While his mother may have been his No. 1 fan, she certainly wasn't alone. "I don't think you guys have any concept of the impact this kid has on a game," Orlando coach Chuck Daly told reporters as the series unfolded. "This was The Allen Iverson Show. He's a tremendous competitor. What he does for the Sixers, I don't think even they realize."

The 76ers' playoff drive stalled in the second round, however, as they were swept by the veteran Indiana Pacers in four hard-fought games. Iverson had 35 points in a Game 1 loss and 25 more in an 89–86 defeat to the Pacers in the decisive fourth game. He averaged 28.8 points for the series, although the Pacers did limit him to .383 shooting. "He's a great, great basketball player ..." Pacers guard Mark Jackson said of Iverson. "No one guy is going to stop him, you just try to contain him and make him work for everything."

The 1999 season was an overwhelmingly positive one for Allen Iverson, but it also had its rocky spots. Although they had smoothed things over by the playoffs, Iverson and Larry Brown feuded just weeks before the post-season. Although both men later assured reporters they had patched things up, this well-publicized incident only fuelled Iverson's critics. Charles Barkley, who had previously referred to the 76ers' guard as "Me-Myself-and-I-verson," attacked him in the April 19 issue of *Sports Illustrated.* "Take Iverson. I can't stand that guy," Barkley said. "He has to show up for practice every day. He has a responsibility to cut the crap and not have some drama with his coach every week. He's showing no respect to anyone, least of all the game."

Iverson responded just as bitingly. "He's nobody," he told the Associated Press, referring to Barkley. Iverson paid much more attention to the advice he'd been given by Detroit Piston senior spokesman Joe Dumars. "He told me not to worry about negative things," Iverson said in a Los Angeles *Times* story. "He told me what to keep and what to throw away. To hear that advice from him, one of the greatest, it makes me feel like I have done something good with my life. His words I will take to my grave."

Craig Esherick believes that Iverson's ability to shut out all the critics has been a key to his success and his survival since high school. When asked for one reason Iverson has made it big in the NBA while others hav failed, the Georgetown coach didn't hesitate. "I thi it's his toughness," Esherick said. "Allen is a great lete, but Allen is also a very, very tough person will not let something said about him or anyt' pull him away from doing what he is attemp

He has incredible physical talent, but the growth he has made proves to me that first, he is a very smart kid; and second, he is very coachable. And his growth is still phenomenal. You can see Allen is a better player every year in the NBA."

Still, Iverson doubts that he has shaken off the "selfish" label. "I don't think so," he says, "because there are always going to be critics out there, guys who will tear me down. Especially reporters who don't really know a thing about the game, never played the game and nine times out of ten, most of them really don't even understand the game. I think that there are going to be a billion people out there that respect my game and love my game and appreciate my game, and a billion people who dislike it. I understand that, so that's what keeps me moving forward."

As the 1999 season concluded, Iverson was clearly among the top players in the NBA. Yet he was not selected for the initial U.S. Dream Team which won the Americas Olympic qualifying tournament in Puerto Rico. This omission was perceived by many as a slight. "I'm not disappointed or upset," Iverson says. "It would be an honour to be on that team, but I just look at it like how it is. This is life and that is how things go in life. I mean, I want to be on that team but I keep moving on. I was incarcerated before and people said that I would never even get to this level. But I am playing on this level and I am happy. I mean, my family is taken care of, my kids are taken care of. I can't ask for more."

ESSENTIAL IVERSON

Name: Allen Iverson
Nicknames: "The Answer", "Bubbachuck"
Position: Guard, Philadelphia 76ers
Born: June 7, 1975; Hampton, VA
Height: 6'   **Weight:** 165 lbs.
High school: Bethel, Hampton, VA
College: Georgetown University, Washington, DC
Drafted: 1996, No.1 overall by Philadelphia 76ers

COLLEGE

As a freshman (1994–95)

30 games; 966 total minutes; .390 from field; .232 from three-point range; .688 from free-throw line; 99 total rebounds; 3.3 rebounds per game; 134 total assists; 4.5 assists per game; 613 total points; 20.4 points per game.

As a sophomore (1995–96)

37 games; 1,213 total minutes; .480 from field; .366 from three-point range; .678 from line; 141 total rebounds; 3.8 rebounds per game; 173 total assists; 4.7 assists per game; 926 total points; 25.0 points per game.

College career (1994–96)

67 games; 2,179 total minutes; .440 from field; .314 from three-point range; .683 from free-throw line; 240 total rebounds; 3.6 rebounds per game; 307 total assists; 4.6 assists per game; 1,539 total points; 23.0 points per game.

College honours

1994–95 — Big East Rookie of the Year; United Press International Rookie of the Year; Big East defensive player of the year; All-Big East Second Team.

1995–96 — Big East defensive player of the year; *The Sporting News* and Associated Press First Team All-American; leading scorer in Big East; unanimous All-Big East First Team.

NBA

1996–97 (Sixers)

76 games; 74 games started; 3,045 total minutes; 40.1 minutes per game; .416 from field; .341 from three-point range; .702 from free-throw line; 312 total rebounds; 4.1 rebounds per

game; 567 total assists; 7.5 assists per game; 24 blocks; 157
steals; 1,787 total points; 23.5 points per game.

1997–98 (Sixers)

80 games; 80 games started; 3,150 total minutes; 39.4 minutes
per game; .461 from field; .298 from three-point range; .729
from free-throw line; 296 total rebounds; 3.7 rebounds per
game; 494 total assists; 6.2 assists per game; 25 blocks; 176
steals; 1,758 total points; 22.0 points per game.

1998–99 (Sixers)

48 games; 48 games started; 1,990 total minutes; 41.5 minutes
per game; .412 from field; .291 from three-point range; .751
from free-throw line; 236 total rebounds; 4.9 rebounds per
game; 223 total assists; 4.6 assists per game; 7 blocks; 110
steals; 1,284 total points; 26.8 points per game.

Career to date (1996–99)

204 games; 202 games started; 8,185 total minutes; 40.1
minutes per game; .431 from field; .318 from three-point range;
.726 from free-throw line; 844 total rebounds; 4.1 rebounds per
game; 1,284 total assists; 6.3 assists per game; 56 blocks; 443
steals; 4,829 total points; 23.7 points per game.

Playoffs to date (1999)

8 games; 8 games started; 358 total minutes; 44.8 minutes per
game; .411 from field; .283 from three-point range; .712 from
free-throw line; 33 total rebounds; 4.1 rebounds per game; 39
total assists; 4.9 assists per game; 2 blocks; 20 steals; 228
points; 28.5 points per game.

NBA honours

1996–97 — NBA Rookie of the Year; NBA All-Rookie First Team;
Rookie All-Star Game MVP.

1998–99 — NBA regular-season scoring leader; All-NBA First
Team.

Sources

Sports Illustrated features, Oct. 25, 1993; and June 13, 1994
Hoop Magazine feature, 1999
Washington *Post*
Associated Press
Washington *Times*
The Sporting News
'ew York *Daily News*

Philadelphia *Daily News*

Chicago *Tribune*

New York *Times*

Los Angeles *Times*

USA Today

Canadian Press

Vancouver *Province*

Georgetown University men's basketball website

NBA.com

Official NBA Register, (regular-season) Guide and Draft Media Guides

STEVE NASH

The NBA is bubbling over with stories of players who have conquered adversity and colourful accounts of dedicated athletes who have overcome incredible odds to realize their dreams. But few were as great a long shot as Steve Nash, the starting point guard for the Dallas Mavericks. In the fall of 1999, Nash began his fourth season in the NBA. Seven years earlier, it would have been difficult to predict that he would get the chance to play even one season.

Nash hailed from western Canada, which is hardly known as a basketball factory. What's more, he came out of high school as a slender, six-foot-two point guard — certainly not the sort of physical specimen that U.S. college coaches are normally seeking in their rare scouting safaris into the Great White North. A third strike against him was the fact he only played a single season of high school basketball. When you add the fact that, prior to Nash being drafted in June of 1996, there were only two Canadians playing in the NBA and that neither had actually played any of his high school ball in Canada, Nash's chances of making it were particularly remote.

In the acclaimed basketball book *Hoop Dreams*, it was estimated that the odds of an American high school player reaching the NBA were 7,600 to one. And this is in the country that produces roughly 95 percent of the NBA's talent pool. Canadian-produced NBA products have been rarer than hairs on Michael Jordan's head. Although one Canadian was drafted in June of 1999 — Washington centre Todd MacCulloch of Winnipeg — only 22 Canadians in total have been selected by NBA teams since 1949. "The odds against Steve making the NBA were huge," says Ken Shields, the former head coach of Canada's national team. "I mean, there's never been a player his size do what he's done in Canada. But he's earned it. He's put in his time. He has the right skill set, physically, mentally, socially, psychologically. He's got the whole package."

Nash's first love was actually soccer. His parents, John and Jean, were from the United Kingdom, and Steve was born in Johannesburg while his father was playing semi-pro soccer in South Africa. The youngster's first documented word, not surprisingly, was "GOAL!" When Steve was still an infant, the Nash family immigrated to Canada, where they eventually ended up in Victoria, British Columbia. Nash grew up in the picturesque capital city of B.C., which sits on the southern tip of Vancouver Island, a 95-minute ferry ride across the Strait of Georgia from the city of Vancouver. From an early age, he was an outstanding athlete in just about every sport he tried including baseball, hockey, lacrosse, golf and, of course, soccer. "Stephen never wanted to play with anything but sporting equipment — ever," recalls his mother Jean. But at the age of 13, while he was attending Arbutus Junior High School, Nash's circle of close friends found themselves drawn into basketball by the glitz and glam of the Michael Jordan era. Nash fell head over hightops for the sport.

While he was still in the eighth grade, Steve decided he would concentrate on making a career out of basketball. The stories of his long hours on the court, shooting in the rain and in near-darkness, have since become legendary in Victoria sports circles. During his junior high and high school summers, he often played basketball for as many as eight hours a day. When other kids went home to eat supper, or out with their friends, Nash hit the playground to work on his regimen. One day, he would assign himself 500 jump shots to be made before he would allow himself to leave the court, the next day it would be 200 free-throws. Although he approached it like work, he viewed it as more of a challenge. But often that challenge meant going home in the dark alone. "I just really fell in love with it from day one," he says now. "I always tried to have a ball in my hand and tried to maximize my time on the court."

Nash was a local standout from the time he first touched a basketball, starring for a small but athletic team at Arbutus that ran all the way to the B.C. junior high school championship game before losing to crosstown rival Spencer. And as the Arbutus players graduated and headed into Mount Douglas Senior Secondary, basketball watchers were predicting success for Nash at the senior level.

Things didn't go smoothly at the suburban Victoria high school, however. Nash began his Grade 11 year nicely by leading Mount Doug's soccer team to the provincial title and being named the most valuable player in the B.C. AAA tournament, but the situation declined rapidly from there. Steve's first report card from Mount Douglas was an eye-opener for his parents. His highest grade was a C-plus and, for the first time ever, he received a D-minus. John and Jean Nash were also shocked to discover their eldest son had 33 absences in his first two-and-a-half months of school. He had always been a steady student and his parents had planned for him to attend university. The way Steve Nash was going, however, he would be lucky to make it to Grade 12, let alone into college. On top of this, Steve and his former Arbutus teammates were clashing with Mount Doug's new basketball coach, Dave Hutchings. During a pre-season meeting about setting individual goals, Steve had informed Hutchings that he aspired to play Division 1 college basketball in the U.S. Hutchings had replied that Steve should perhaps think about adopting some more realistic goals.

With their son reeling academically and unhappy with his situation on the basketball court, John and Jean Nash decided to transfer Steve to St. Michaels University School (SMUS), a nearby private institution with an emphasis on academics as well as a strong sports program.

While critics whispered that the transfer was simply a veiled recruiting move by SMUS, Nash's parents were making the change for one reason only. Their son badly needed academic structure and discipline if he hoped to attend university. And St. Michaels would provide that, eventually raising Nash's academic performance so that he qualified for post-secondary entrance. But the move also came with a major drawback. High school transfer rules, designed to prevent schools from recruiting athletes, required Nash to forfeit his entire Grade 11 basketball season. This was a tremendous blow and it would ultimately hamper Nash in his search for a U.S. college scholarship. Steve was left with only one high school season in which to make his mark, both on the court and with college coaches.

The on-court challenge was the easiest one. The Nash-led St. Michaels University School Blue Devils stormed their way to a 50–4 record and the B.C. AAA high school championship. For the season, Nash was clearly the outstanding prep player in the province, averaging 21.3 points, 11.2 assists and 9.1 rebounds — nearly a triple-double — per game. But catching the attention of U.S. schools proved a much more frustrating challenge. Prior to his senior season, Nash had approached SMUS head coach Ian Hyde-Lay, asking him for help in his search for a scholarship. "I'll do everything I possibly can," Hyde-Lay replied, "but you've got to realize that with these big U.S. schools, they're already looking to sign the top high school players as they finish their grade 11 seasons or even earlier. You haven't even *had* a grade 11 season." Nevertheless, the energetic private-school coach and teacher set out on an ambitious letter-writing campaign to National Collegiate Athletic Association (NCAA) Division 1 schools, contacting 30 programs. His list included every school in the Pac-10 and a cross-section of the better basketball schools across the U.S. His letters referred interested colleges to Canadian national-team coach Ken Shields, who had invited a barely 17-year-old Nash to scrimmage with his team the previous spring at the University of Victoria.

A few schools responded to those initial letters from Hyde-Lay, calling Shields and then requesting videotape of Steve Nash from his high school coach. Among the interested programs were Miami, Virginia, Indiana, Long Beach State, Clemson, Utah and Santa Clara, a smaller Division One school located in California's Bay Area. Hyde-Lay helped string together a crude highlight tape of one of Nash's early-season games and forwarded it to these schools. The tape, which showed Nash weaving through a series of defenders with ease, created a stir at the Santa Clara basketball office. In fact, coach Dick Davey remembers hearing a hearty chuckle coming from the office where fellow assistant Scott Gradin was watching the tape. "You gotta look at this," Gradin had chuckled. "This guy makes people fall down."

Although the tape wasn't enough evidence to convince Davey that Nash was a legitimate prospect, it did make him want to see more. Santa Clara requested another tape from SMUS, which Hyde-Lay provided. This tape showed more game action. And what Dick Davey, then a 15-year assistant with the Broncos, saw reminded him of a young Bobby Hurley. "Oh boy," Davey found himself thinking. "This kid's pretty good."

The Broncos were virtually alone in their admiration for Steve Nash, at least when it came to American schools. Initial interest from Indiana, Long Beach State and Virginia eventually dried up. By the first week of March in Nash's senior year, Santa Clara was the lone U.S. school still showing any interest. "It's unlucky," Hyde-Lay thought at the time. "But for a six-foot-one white kid from Canada, that's probably just the way it is."

Santa Clara head coach Carroll Williams dispatched Dick Davey to Vancouver to check out Steve Nash in person during the 1992 B.C. AAA boys' tournament. As soon as Davey saw this kid in action, he knew Nash was capable of playing south of the border. In fact, as the game continued in the PNE Agrodome, Davey found himself scouring the arena's mostly empty seats, wondering if any major U.S. colleges had caught the scent of this prospect.

Fortunately for Santa Clara, none had. And less than a month later, Steve Nash's name was on a letter of intent to accept a basketball scholarship to the Bay Area school. "It wasn't a case of being an Einstein," Dick Davey would later tell *Sports Illustrated* of the recruiting process. "There was no magic wand. I just got very lucky." As he headed for the NCAA that fall, Steve Nash felt the same way. Santa Clara wasn't Indiana or Duke or North Carolina, but it was a U.S. college basketball program that was willing to give him an opportunity. And for that he felt both grateful and relieved.

Nash's freshman year at the small, private university just south of San Francisco didn't live up to his hopes, however — at least not early on. He found himself desperately homesick and he was having trouble in practice with Dick Davey, who over the summer had succeeded Carroll Williams as the Broncos' head coach. To add to his troubles, in early November Nash came down with a severe case of the flu and had to be hospitalized overnight. When he returned to practice, he was weak and he struggled mightily just to advance the ball upcourt against Santa Clara's starting point guard John Woolery. His confidence was slipping and he wanted to go home. At the same time, he knew he couldn't. Not if he wanted to keep his dream alive.

It was his early relationship with Davey, the man who had recruited him, that Nash found to be the most difficult adjustment. The coach was demanding and often vocally critical, especially of his young freshman. The relationship between Nash and Davey would eventually improve, however, and so would Nash's on-court fortunes. John Woolery went down with an injury midway through the season and Nash was forced into the Broncos' starting lineup for three games. That stint helped him regain his confidence and set him up for what would be a terrific finish to the season. After averaging just 5.8 points over the team's first 16 games, Nash would average 11.3 over the final 11. He would end his freshman year with 252 points, the most for a Santa Clara rookie since 1978.

It was in the West Coast Conference (WCC) tournament that Steve Nash would really make his mark, however. In the tournament final, against heavily favoured Pepperdine, Steve scored a game-high 23 points on five-for-six shooting from three-point range. The 73–63 win lifted the Broncos into the prestigious NCAA Tournament for the first time since 1987 and Nash was selected as the first freshman MVP in WCC Tournament history. Delirious fans at the University of San Francisco held up signs saying: "We are NASHty!"

"These are high-pressure games with a lot at stake. And for an 18-year-old freshman to be doing that well under this kind of pressure ... I think we're seeing something very unique," said ESPN analyst and former Laker great Kareem Abdul-Jabbar. Santa Clara's spring magic wasn't finished, however. During the first round of the NCAA Tournament, the Broncos became just the second No. 15 seed to knock off a No. 2. They stunned the powerful Arizona Wildcats and their star-studded lineup — one that included future NBAers Damon Stoudamire, Khalid Reeves and Chris Mills. Santa Clara's super freshman Steve Nash finished the game with 10 points, including six straight free-throws to ice the 64–61 victory down the stretch.

Nash's freshman finale was just an appetizer of what was to come over the rest of his career at Santa Clara. As a sophomore, he averaged 14.6 points as the Broncos struggled to a 13–14 record. But it was his junior season when he defined himself as a legitimate NBA prospect by upping his scoring average to 20.9 points, adding 6.4 assists per game and leading the Broncos back into the NCAA Tournament. The standout season also earned him the West Coast Conference Player of the Year award.

Spurred on by his success at Santa Clara, Nash's dedication to improving his individual skills also grew. Some days, he dribbled a tennis ball across campus to hone his ballhandling. Some nights, he asked Broncos' manager Antonio Veloso to unlock Toso Pavilion so that he and teammate Jason Sedlock could play two-on-two with the reserve freshman until the wee hours of the morning. "Steve works harder than anybody I've ever played with, by far," says John Woolery, his former Broncos teammate. "And he's never afraid to ask someone else how to get better."

By the time Nash's senior season arrived, the hype was beginning to build around this heretofore little-known point guard from Canada. It continued to climb after November, when Nash was superb in the Broncos' 78–69 upset of heavily-favoured UCLA in the first round of the Maui Invitational. His profile hit an all-time high in early December 1995, when Nash was featured in a five-page spread in *Sports Illustrated* entitled: "Little Magic." In this article, the legend of his non-recruitment by all but one U.S. college program was extended to nearly mythic proportions.

Dealing with the defensive double-teams and trying to live up to the expectations wasn't easy during Nash's senior season. But despite facing defences designed purely to stop him, battling nagging injuries and seeing NBA scouts at every game, Nash finished the year averaging 17 points and six assists to earn his second straight conference MVP award. What's more, he led the Broncos into their third NCAA Tournament of his four-year career. Santa Clara even staged another post-season upset. The Broncos, led by Steve's 28-point, 12-assist effort, beat an athletic Maryland squad 91–79 in Tempe, Arizona. The banner headline in the next day's San Jose *Mercury News* would read, simply: "MONSTER NASH."

Nash's transformation from a high school senior practically begging for a scholarship into an NCAA star was remarkable. He finished his career at Santa Clara averaging 14.9 points, 4.5 assists and 3.1 rebounds. The player only one U.S. school had wanted was now an honourable mention All-American and Santa Clara's all-time assists leader with 510 over four years. He would finish as the Broncos' finest-ever three-point and free-throw shooter and wind up third on Santa Clara's all-time scoring (1,689 points) and steals (147) lists.

When Steve Nash played his final regular-season home game in front of a packed Toso Pavilion, his school paid him the ultimate tribute by having the Canadian national anthem sung during the pre-game ceremony. "To coach Steve has been probably the ultimate for a coach, at least from my point of view," Dick Davey said as the finest player in Santa Clara's history graduated. "He's the epitome of what a coach wants. He makes the game so much easier for me because he can dictate what we do out there with intelligence and skill … We've had a premier, unbelievable player in our program. Hopefully someday we'll have another chance to have somebody like him."

Nash didn't have much time to dwell on his university career, however. During a six-week period following the Broncos' second-round NCAA Tournament loss to Kansas, he would work out individually for 10 NBA teams. Estimates of where he would go in the draft ranged from as high as No. 5 to the second round, depending on who you listened to. But after a strong showing at the Nike Desert Classic in Phoenix, Arizona, most agreed that Steve Nash would go reasonably early in the June 26, 1996 draft at East Rutherford, New Jersey.

Nash was eventually chosen 15th by the Phoenix Suns, making him the highest drafted Canadian ever, beating centre Bill Wennington who was a No. 16 pick of the Dallas Mavericks in 1985, and guard Leo Rautins who had gone at No. 17 to the Philadelphia 76ers in 1983. The historical significance of the pick was apparently lost on Canadian television rights-holder YTV, however, as the network left its draft coverage prior to Steve's selection to show an episode of *The Flintstones*.

Moments after NBA commissioner David Stern announced his name in New Jersey, Steve was walking on air. "This is just a dream come true and it's unbelievable. There were so many days growing up when I said to myself: 'There's no way I'm going back to the gym right now.' Then, two minutes later, I'd say: 'Yeah, you're going to the gym, so that you can sit here on a day like this.' If on five percent of those days, I had decided to just stay at home, I wouldn't be where I am today."

The feeling of euphoria wasn't universally shared by Phoenix fans, however. The Suns announced their pick to a draft-night party at America West Arena, where the fans booed the selection of the relatively unknown point guard from Canada. Phoenix had bypassed Syracuse University Final Four hero John Wallace in favour of Nash and clearly some supporters were disappointed. "I'm glad they booed," Nash said. "It showed that they're passionate about their team. I probably would have booed myself, too."

Ironically, Steve Nash would go on to become one of Suns' more popular players during his first two seasons in Phoenix. Once again, however, the odds seemed stacked against the young Canadian. He was coming to a franchise with incumbent all-star Kevin Johnson entrenched at the point. As well, veteran Sam Cassell had just been obtained from Houston in a multi-player swap for Charles Barkley. Johnson would be plagued by injuries, which allowed Nash to get some early playing time in his rookie season, including a brilliant "homecoming" performance on November 14 in Vancouver, when he racked up 17 points, 12 assists, seven rebounds and three steals in his first NBA start. He was also selected to play in the NBA's Rookie All-Star Game. But after late December of 1996, when the Suns made another blockbuster trade to Dallas for star point guard Jason Kidd, Nash's future in Phoenix grew murkier. He would end his rookie season averaging just 3.3 points and 2.1 assists in limited time off the bench.

Nash continued to work hard in his second season, forcing Phoenix head coach Danny Ainge to find him more playing time. During the 1997–98 season, he averaged better than 20 minutes, 9.1 points and 3.4 assists in an effective backup role to Kidd. Ainge also liked his hustle, his court sense and his shooting skills enough to sometimes play the under-sized Nash at the shooting guard spot. He ended his second season in the NBA as the Suns' top three-point shooter (.415) and 13th among the NBA's long-range bombers.

Nevertheless, with Jason Kidd firmly established as the No. 1 point guard in Phoenix, it was obvious that Steve Nash wasn't going to get a chance to run the Suns' offence on a regular basis. In the summer of 1998, after he had opted not to sign a contract extension that would have tied him to Phoenix, the Suns made Nash part of a draft-day trade. Phoenix sent Steve to the Dallas Mavericks for forward Martin Muursepp, swingman Bubba Wells, forward Pat Garrity and a 1999 first-round draft choice. The trade surprised casual NBA observers who certainly hadn't been bowled over by Nash's numbers in his first two seasons. But insiders weren't shocked. No less than nine teams had made overtures to the Suns about Nash.

Steve was in England, visiting relatives, when the deal was made. He found it difficult to contain his enthusiasm, even over the long-distance line. Finally, he would get a chance to pilot his own NBA team. The deal would also make Nash an extremely wealthy young man. Although his first NBA contract, worth $3.2 million U.S. over three seasons, had long since secured his financial future, the Mavericks would sweeten the pot considerably by signing their new acquisition to a six-year, $33-million U.S. extension just after the NBA labour lockout was lifted. It seemed everything was falling into place for Steve Nash as the 1999 season opened.

Perhaps it was trying to justify that huge new contract. Perhaps it was the result of trying to win over the Mavericks' fans all at once. Perhaps it was the intensely compacted 50-game NBA schedule. For whatever reason, in 1999 Steve Nash experienced the worst season of his pro career. Normally a superb shooter, Nash struggled to find his range during his first season with the Mavs. Shots that felt fine when they left his hand mysteriously rimmed out. He finished the year shooting just .363 from the field and .374 from three-point range, the poorest numbers of his career and considerably off his form of the previous year with Phoenix. For the season, he would average 7.9 points and 5.5 assists in 31.7 minutes per game, clearly not the kind of numbers he or the Mavericks fans expected.

"I think I tried to put too much pressure on myself at the start of the season," Nash told the Dallas *Morning News.* "I wanted everyone to know I was a good player, and I wanted to impress the home fans. I know I can shoot the ball better than I have, but I wasn't relaxing."

The season was also a struggle physically. Anything that could go wrong, did. Nash came into the year recovering from *plantar fasciitis,* a painful heel injury. Then he injured his back during a hard fall in the pre-season. He broke his nose early in the schedule before coming down with a respiratory ailment that sapped his energy.

A back injury, which team doctors believe he has been playing with for years, caused him to miss the final 10 games of the Mavericks' season and also nearly kept him from playing over the summer with the Canadian Olympic team in Puerto Rico as it attempted to qualify for the 2000 Sydney Games.

But the thing that hurt most was that the Mavericks were losing. Head coach and General Manager Don Nelson had promised fans that the team would be a playoff contender and that new acquisition Steve Nash would help lead the way. But the Mavs began the season 1–8 and were out of the playoff race from the start. They would finish at 19–31 and face the hostility of disappointed fans. Nobody felt that hostility more than Nash, who had become a lightning rod for fan disenchantment. During an 88–78 loss to visiting Houston on March 24, a game in which he went 1-for-10 from the field, Nash was booed by the home Reunion Arena crowd every time he touched the ball in the second half. The reaction stunned teammates and even opponents.

It also shocked Steve Nash, who had been a fan favourite throughout his college and NBA careers. "The day it happened was kind of bizarre," he says. "But the next day I got over it. You just don't expect to be singled out like that when nobody on the team is playing well. But I understand it. The fans pay money to watch us play and they have every right to voice their opinions." Others weren't so understanding. "I'm very disappointed in the Dallas fans," Houston forward Charles Barkley told reporters after the game. "Why don't they send him down to Houston? We'll take him."

Nash isn't going anywhere, however. Despite reported pre-draft trade interest for the point guard from both Minnesota and Toronto, Nelson still seems confident that the player he obtained in 1998 will shine in

Dallas. And with six more years left on his contract, the Canadian long shot figures to be a fixture in Texas.

"There's going to be a point," he promises, "where this will all be forgotten and this will all be just a bump in the road. I'm willing to accept responsibility — I haven't played well. I'm subject to criticism. That's fine and I understand it. All I can do is work hard on every aspect of my game … You've just got to do the things you've always done and don't let your life hinge on shots going in or out."

That philosophy worked for Nash during the summer of 1999, when he led an unheralded group of Canadian players to a coveted spot in the 2000 Sydney Olympics. Nash was outstanding during July's Americas zone qualifying tournament in San Juan, particularly in the key semifinal showdown against the host Puerto Ricans when he helped lock up Canada's first Olympic men's basketball berth in 12 years. In that pressure-packed game, Nash made five of seven three-point attempts, scored 26 points and added a team-high eight rebounds as the Canadians stunned the home side on the hostile floor of Roberto Clemente Coliseum.

Prior to the tournament, few had given the Canadians much chance of qualifying considering there were 10 teams competing for only two Olympic berths and one of those spots had been virtually conceded to the high-powered Americans. Former national team coach Ken Shields called it the biggest win ever for Canadian basketball. And current head coach Jay Triano described Nash's effort as the biggest clutch performance in national team history.

All Steve Nash cared about was the win, the result of a selfless effort by a group of players who had fought tooth and nail for each other. There's nothing quite like the thrill of a long shot beating overwhelming odds.

"This is just an incredible feeling," Nash said. "I just hope the kids back home were proud watching it, because we were all proud to be playing for Canada."

NASH NUMBERS

Name: Stephen John Nash
Position: Point guard, Dallas Mavericks
Height: 6'3" **Weight:** 195 lbs.
Born: February 7, 1974; Johannesburg, South Africa
High schools: Mount Douglas Senior Secondary and St. Michaels University School, both Victoria, BC
College: Santa Clara University, Santa Clara, CA
Drafted: 1996, No. 15 overall by Phoenix Suns

COLLEGE
As a freshman (1992–93)
31 games; 743 total minutes; .424 from field; .408 from three-point range; .825 from free-throw line; 79 total rebounds; 2.5 rebounds per game; 67 total assists; 2.2 assists per game; 252 total points; 8.1 points per game.
As a sophomore (1993–94)
26 games; 778 total minutes; .414 from field; .399 from three-point range; .831 from free-throw line; 65 total rebounds; 2.5 rebounds per game; 95 total assists; 3.7 assists per game; 380 total points; 14.6 points per game.
As a junior (1994–95)
27 games; 902 total minutes; .444 from field; .454 from three-point range; .879 from free-throw line; 102 total rebounds; 3.8 rebounds per game; 174 total assists; 6.4 assists per game; 565 total points; 20.9 points per game.
As a senior (1995–96)
29 games; 979 total minutes; .430 from field; .344 from three-point range; .894 from free-throw line; 102 total rebounds; 3.5 rebounds per game; 174 total assists; 6.0 assists per game; 492 total points; 17.0 points per game.
College career (1992–96)
113 games played; 3,402 minutes played; .430 from field; .401

from three-point range; .867 from free-throw line; 348 total rebounds; 3.5 rebounds per game; 510 total assists; 4.5 assists per game; 1,689 points; 14.9 points per game.

College honours

1992–93 — West Coast Conference (WCC) Tournament MVP.

1994–95 — WCC Player of the Year; John Wooden Award candidate.

1995–96 — WCC Player of the Year; John Wooden Award candidate; Associated Press and United States Basketball Writers Association honourable mention All-American.

College records

Santa Clara's all-time career leader in assists (510) and free-throw percentage (.861); third in all-time Santa Clara career scoring (1,689 points).

NBA

1996–97 (Suns)

65 games; 2 games started; 684 total minutes; 10.5 minutes per game; .423 from field; .418 from three-point range; .824 from free-throw line; 63 total rebounds; 1.0 rebounds per game; 138 total assists; 2.1 assists per game; 0 blocks; 20 steals; 213 total points; 3.3 points per game.

1997–98 (Suns)

76 games; 9 games started; 1,664 total minutes; 21.9 minutes per game; .459 from field; .415 from three-point range; .860 from free-throw line; 160 total rebounds; 2.1 rebounds per game; 262 total assists; 3.4 assists per game; 4 blocks; 63 steals; 691 total points; 9.1 points per game.

1998–99 (Mavericks)

40 games; 40 games started; 1,269 total minutes; 31.7 minutes per game; .363 from field; .374 from three-point range; .826 from free-throw line; 114 total rebounds; 2.9 rebounds per game; 219 total assists; 5.5 assists per game; 2 blocks; 37 steals; 315 total points; 7.9 points per game.

Career to date (1996-99)

181 games; 51 games started; 3,617 total minutes; 20 minutes per game; .425 from field; .402 from three-point range; .842 from free-throw line; 337 total rebounds; 1.9 rebounds per game; 619 total assists; 3.4 assists per game; 6 blocks; 120 steals; 1,219 total points; 6.7 points per game.

Playoffs to date

8 games played; 1 game started; 66 total minutes; 8.3 minutes per game; .370 from field; .222 from three-point range; .625 from free-throw line; 11 total rebounds; 1.4 rebounds per game; 8 total assists; 1 assist per game; 1 block; 3 steals; 27 total points; 3.4 points per game.

NBA honours

1996–97 — NBA Rookie All-Star Game.

1997–98 — Finished third, teamed with Michele Timms of the WNBA's Phoenix Mercury, in All-Star 2ball competition.

Sources

Long Shot: Steve Nash's Journey to the NBA (Polestar, 1996)

Victoria *Times Colonist*

Sports Illustrated feature, Dec. 11, 1995

Vancouver *Sun*

Vancouver *Province*

San Jose *Mercury News*

Dallas *Morning News*

NBA.com

Official NBA Register, (regular-season) Guide and Draft Media Guide

MICHAEL OLOWOKANDI

The telephone rang just as Tony Marcopulos was beginning to tuck into his salami and cheese on sourdough.
And although the tasty sandwich beckoned, the phone
simply had to be answered. That was the house rule in
the men's basketball office at University of the Pacific.
Whenever the secretary was at lunch, one of the assistant coaches was required to cover. As Pacific head coach
Bob Thomason was fond of saying: "You never know
when a seven-footer is going to call."

Marcopulos was pretty sure he knew: Never, that's
when. Still, the phone was ringing now. He answered.

"Hello, my name is Michael Olowokandi," said a
voice with a thick British accent, the words tumbling
out so rapidly that Marcopulos could barely understand
them. "I'm seven feet tall, 265 pounds," the voice continued. "I'm from London. I want to play basketball."

It was April 3, 1995, and Marcopulos would have
been forgiven for thinking somebody was playing a be-
lated April Fool's trick. Seven-footers from across the
ocean — seven-footers from anywhere, for that matter
— didn't just phone Pacific out of the blue. That might
happen at Duke or UCLA but not at this Northern
California private university with less than 4,000 students and a modest Division 1 basketball program. Still,
Marcopulos listened, intrigued by the long-distance voice

on the other end. It belonged to a well-spoken, 20-year-old university student from London, England, who had apparently picked Pacific at random out of a *Peterson's Guide to American Colleges*. The polite young man explained that he wanted an opportunity to play U.S. college basketball and had decided to try to create that opportunity for himself.

"We don't have any scholarships available," Marcopulos told him.

"Well, that's OK," Olowokandi replied. "I can pay my own way."

"OK, we'll take you," answered the Pacific assistant. "You can come." And so began one of the strangest stories in hoops history. Michael Olowokandi, who had only ever played the game recreationally, was on his way to the NBA.

Of course, in the beginning, the NBA was so far away it was barely a concept for Olowokandi. It was a fleeting dream world that he knew only from the Michael Jordan videos he had seen in England. But it was a dream world he wanted to be part of. Olowokandi had just turned 20 and he knew he was running out of time. He reasoned he would need to find a school to which he could transfer his academic credits and where he could try out for the basketball team. Finding a National Collegiate Athletic Association (NCAA) school that would help him do that was just the first step.

Born in 1975 in Lagos, Nigeria, Olowokandi had moved with his parents to London when he was just three years old. He had always been tall — in fact, he grew six inches in one two-year span and was fully six-foot-eight before he reached his 16th birthday. He eventually developed into a strapping, athletic seven-footer who played the traditional English sports of soccer, rugby, cricket and track and field during his boarding school days at Newlands Manor School in East Sussex.

After prep school, Olowokandi had moved on to study mechanical engineering at Brunel University in Uxbridge, which did not sponsor any athletic programs. While studying there, he and a couple of friends had watched the video of the basketball movie *White Men Can't Jump*. Not long after seeing that movie, they spied a basketball lying in the corner of the school's sports equipment storage room. They took it outside to toss around and dribble and, almost immediately, Olowokandi knew he had found his game. A strong all-around athlete, Olowokandi had always been blessed with the ability to jump and run. But with basketball, he quickly discovered that he could finally use his towering height and reach to supreme advantage. He could also dunk with ease. And wasn't that pretty much all the game entailed?

His friends' interest in the sport quickly waned, but Olowokandi found that playing basketball made him feel good. The game, especially the way it was packaged and promoted by the NBA, was something intriguing, something he wanted to be a part of and, unlike other sports, it never got boring or old. Soon he was playing recreationally every chance he got. The seed had been planted and, before long, it would lead to his fateful cold call to the University of the Pacific.

Once Olowokandi had made that first move toward the NCAA, the ball was in Tony Marcopulos' court. The veteran Pacific assistant coach spent the next two to three months checking out his English prospect, making sure his credits from Brunel University would transfer, that he would pass the SAT exam, and that Olowokandi would indeed be declared eligible by the NCAA. The extensive legwork included 50 to 60 long-distance telephone calls between Marcopulos and Olowokandi. But the assistant coach enjoyed chatting with the personable young mystery man from England. And the way Marcopulos saw it, his school had absolutely nothing to lose. The Tigers weren't even using a scholarship on this kid. "The worst thing that could happen," Marcopulos thought, "is if he's no good, then we've got a big old seven-footer on campus."

Four months after the initial phone call, Michael Olowokandi arrived at Pacific. He soon had his future teammates buzzing in anticipation of the coming season. In fact, some players who had caught a glimpse of him during informal pickup games seemed almost frightened of this newcomer because he was so big. Olowokandi was a physical specimen of a type not usually seen around the Stockton, California, campus.

A few days after he arrived, Olowokandi joined Marcopulos and other coaches for his first individual workout in the gym. He certainly looked like a pro. Everybody on staff was eager to see this guy play. "Go to the low block and let's see what you can do," Marcopulos told the newcomer. Olowokandi looked puzzled. He wasn't familiar with the term. And it quickly became obvious he hadn't had much in the way of basketball schooling. Not only was he unaware of basic terminology like "baseline" and "key," he also didn't catch, pass or dribble the ball properly. Almost everything was done in an awkward, tentative fashion. And while he was a physically imposing young man, he wasn't in good shape. Certainly not in NCAA basketball shape. Marcopulos was disappointed. "He's horrible," the assistant thought to himself. "He's absolutely the worst (college) basketball player I've seen in my life."

Head coach Bob Thomason, just beginning his eighth season at the helm of the Tigers, shared in the grim assessment. When his longtime assistant had told him about Olowokandi, he'd been skeptical. "A seven-footer, who wants to pay his own way to our school?" Thomason thought. "Yeah, I'm sure this is going to work out *real* good." Still, there had been no gamble for Pacific and Thomason had been curious to see his new overseas project in action. But after this initial workout, he was seriously wondering whether Olowokandi could ever become a college player. The kid had a nice little touch with his hook shot and he certainly had size and athletic ability. But basketball basics American players mastered in grade school were completely new concepts to the raw seven-footer. His entire first day in the gym would be spent going over terminology, rules and markings on the basketball court. This was going to be a bigger project than anybody had anticipated.

Olowokandi's numbers in his first season at Pacific would do little to shake that "project" label. Because everything was so new, he was often thinking his way around the court instead of simply reacting as other players did. Often when an official blew his whistle, Olowokandi didn't know what to do or where to go. The result was a tentative player who, despite his height and obvious physical attributes, didn't even get off the bench some nights. For his first season at Pacific — he began his career as a sophomore under NCAA transfer rules — Olowokandi would average only 10.3 minutes, four points and 3.4 rebounds a game.

But although it wasn't reflected immediately, tremendous growth was occurring inside Olowokandi. Teammates and coaches were continually taking him aside during drills and explaining things to him. Fellow big men Vic Trierweiler and Rayne Mahaffey alternately pounded Olowokandi and patiently taught him the game from a player's standpoint. "Our players did an absolutely wonderful job with Michael," Thomason says now.

"When it was obvious he was frustrated during drills, his teammates would help him out. And, eventually, Michael would beat those guys out for playing time."

Sometimes, it was a struggle for a young man from a completely different culture to fit in. Olowokandi didn't understand the common colloquialisms of a North American locker room. When teammates would jokingly rib him, he initially took it as a serious personal challenge worth fighting over. For the most part, however, the other Pacific players found him a bit of a mystery. He was shy, but well-spoken and clearly intelligent. And until he learned he could trust his teammates, he kept to himself.

Meanwhile, the coaches noticed something unique about their project. Unlike U.S.-raised players, he had no preconceived ideas about how he should or shouldn't play. Nor did he have an attitude. He was a clean slate or, as Marcopulos would say, "a blank tape." They also noticed that, unlike the vast majority of players, Olowokandi could receive instruction and almost immediately add it to his game arsenal. He might not always duplicate the proper technique in practice, but somehow he could do it under the spotlight of game conditions. And he was a tireless worker. For these reasons, and because he was a rare seven-footer with obvious athletic ability, nobody gave up on him.

What was required wasn't easy on anybody, however. Olowokandi needed hours of individual work with big-man coach Ron Verlin on basics such as simple jump stops, balance and pivoting. Verlin and other coaches would spend up to two hours a night feeding him balls in the post. Fortunately, Olowokandi seemed ready and eager for all the work they could dish out. "To his credit, Mike admitted that he didn't know the game," Marcopulos says now. "He was very coachable, open to anything we had to say. He's kind of redefined for me as a coach what 'coachability' is."

Still, the Pacific coaches wondered whether Olowokandi was competitive enough to become a serious player. Sometimes it seemed as though he lacked fire and, early on at least, his pride prevented him from taking chances. During one game in his first season, when Verlin told Olowokandi to get ready to play during the final minutes, the big man declined to go in. "Coach, I don't want to go in," Olowokandi told Verlin. "I don't feel comfortable going in and the other guys are doing a good job." Late into his first season of American college basketball, there were plenty of questions surrounding Michael Olowokandi.

Although that first season was mostly a trial by fire, a few things happened near the end of Pacific's schedule that made coaches, teammates and fans sit up and take notice. Over the season's final nine games, Olowokandi averaged 6.4 points and 5.4 rebounds and he blocked five shots in one February game against Nevada. But it was during a matchup against UC Irvine, a team headed for first place in the conference, that the turning point arrived. Olowokandi suddenly broke out for a 17-point, nine-rebound effort in just 17 minutes on the court. What's more, he dominated a game for the first time since arriving at Stockton. That night, the "project" served up an appetizer of things to come. "It was like a lightbulb went on," recalls former Tigers teammate Adam Jacobsen, now an assistant coach at Pacific. "In that game, it was like he saw his potential, of where he could go if he worked hard ... You kind of had a feeling — everybody was really excited for the next season."

During the summer between his sophomore and junior years at Pacific, the Tigers and Olowokandi made a tour to the West Coast of Canada, playing club and university teams. Olowokandi didn't perform particularly well during the trip and the coaching staff let him know it. "You're still our third-string centre," Thomason told him after the trip. But Michael Olowokandi had other plans. He hadn't flown thousands of miles and turned his life upside down just to give up when things got tough. He was beginning to realize what kind of commitment it would take to become more than just a seven-foot curiosity from England — to become a real player. And unbeknownst to those at Pacific, he was ready to make that commitment. Prior to returning home to London, he boldly told Marcopulos: "I'm going to be an NBA player." The assistant bit his tongue, resisting the urge to say "You're absolutely nuts." Instead, he and other Pacific coaches helped set up Olowokandi with a weight workout schedule, a running routine, skills drills and endless film review. Marcopulos even picked up a video of the NBA's 50 all-time greatest players, to lend their project some perspective.

There was also the little matter of addressing the rules of the game. Olowokandi still didn't know them all. There had been times as a sophomore when he had been caught standing at the free-throw line, waiting for a second attempt, while his teammates and opponents were backpedalling the other way. He was so proud that he was sometimes unwilling to ask his teammates or coaches for clarification. Marcopulos was aware of this, so he had Olowokandi work as a scorekeeper for high school basketball camp games between his sophomore and junior years. It was yet another way for the big guy to further his crash course in the game. Marcopulos still had serious doubts about whether all this effort would ever pay off, but Olowokandi's potential made it worthwhile. "And who am I to take his dream away?" the assistant thought at the time.

Marcopulos' mind began to slowly change before the seven-footer's junior season began. After several weeks in England, Olowokandi returned to Pacific a new player. He had clearly followed the off-season regimens laid out for him by the coaches. He was stronger, more determined and in much better shape. The difference in just one year was incredible. "That first practice back, it was clear he was our starting centre," Marcopulos recalls. "It wasn't even close." From that point on, Thomason and his staff believed that Olowokandi was ready to make the most of his talent and his opportunity. And the proof wasn't long in coming. In the first game of his junior season, he pumped in 25 points in a one-point loss to Fresno State.

The improvement was difficult to miss. After that season-opening loss to Fresno State, Olowokandi led Pacific to victory in its next 16 games, the second-longest winning streak in school history. But Olowokandi's college coming-out party — when he really got people outside of Pacific to take notice — was a December 1996 game in his junior season against the powerful Georgetown Hoyas at Las Vegas. Playing in only his second season of competitive basketball, he completely dominated the paint against the physical Hoyas, scoring 16 points, adding 14 rebounds and holding Georgetown's star centre Jahidi White, an NBA draft prospect, off the scoresheet altogether.

"It's incredible," Bob Thomason told the Associated Press late in Olowokandi's junior season. "I've never seen anyone improve as much as he has in a year's period." Unfortunately, Olowokandi's junior season would be cut short by a strained ligament in his right knee and an ankle injury that kept him out of all but three league contests and allowed him to appear in only 19 games altogether for the Tigers. Despite the physical setbacks, he managed to average 10.9 points, 6.6 rebounds and 1.7 blocks for the season, mammoth increases over his first-year numbers. And he returned from his injuries in time to help lead Pacific into the prestigious NCAA Tournament for the first time since 1979, a feat that helped Bob Thomason land his second Big West Conference Coach of the Year award.

The excitement at Pacific over Olowokandi's senior year was palpable. Despite the school's modest size, the Tigers and Olowokandi would draw average crowds of 4,946 fans during the 1997–98 campaign. It was the first time in school history that every game in the 6,150-seat Spanos Center would draw more than 4,000 spectators. The Tigers would reward their fans by running their homecourt winning streak to 30 games, the second-longest in the nation behind Kansas. The Tigers' rise was mirrored by the incredible improvement of their centre. The summer before his senior season, Olowokandi had attended Pete Newell's Big Man Camp in Hawaii, annual sessions to which the top young centres in basketball are invited to hone their skills against one another. His group at camp included Brad Millard of Saint Mary's, Stanford's Tim Young and Brad Miller of Purdue. Olowokandi had more than held his own during this camp and returned to Pacific feeling he could score at will on anybody.

In his senior year, Olowokandi faced Tim Young and his heavily favoured Stanford team. Prior to the game, Olowokandi told Verlin: "I will kick his (Young's) butt tonight." Then he went out and proved it, piling up 26 points against Young, most of them on tough shots, along with 11 rebounds. "A lot of NBA scouts were convinced then," says Thomason. Olowokandi would lead Pacific in rebounding in 30 of its 33 games and in scoring 25 times. Against Boise State in February he piled up 35 points and he had a career-best 21 rebounds against UC Irvine the same month. Against Cal-Santa Barbara, he recorded seven blocks in a single game. Led by Olowokandi, the Tigers finished the season at 23–10, reached the Big West Conference championship game for the second straight season and played in the National Invitational Tournament (NIT) for the first time in school history. Over Olowokandi's final two years at the school, Pacific rolled up 47 wins, the most ever for the Tigers in a two-year span.

As Olowokandi's prodigious progression at Pacific continued, Thomason began to force his former project out of his comfort zone. He didn't just root Olowokandi to the low block as some coaches might have, but instead worked on making him a more versatile player. He made his centre dribble and pass the ball on the fast break almost every day in practice. Thomason and his staff pushed Olowokandi, even when he didn't really want to be pushed. The Pacific coaches made him rise early to jog and Thomason continued to pull Olowokandi from games when he settled for the turna-round jumper rather than going hard to the basket. In the middle of his senior year, when Thomason thought Olowokandi needed to be in better shape, he had the seven-footer run wind sprints after practice.

All of that helped and, combined with Olowokandi's work ethic, it paid big dividends in his senior year. Olowokandi would average 22.2 points, 11.2 rebounds and 2.9 blocks — all conference bests — and shoot almost 61 percent from the field in his final college season. He would be among the nation's top 10 players in four categories — scoring, rebounding, blocks and field-goal percentage. The player who barely got off the bench in his first year would finish his amazing stint at Pacific as the Big West Conference Player of the Year and an honorable mention All-

American. Before Olowokandi graduated from Pacific with a degree in economics, fellow students were tracking him down on campus for autographs.

Meanwhile, slowly but surely, Olowokandi was becoming the buzz player of the 1998 NBA draft, with a ready-made pro nickname — The Kandi Man — that had caught on at Pacific. He had gone from being a sophomore who didn't even register a blip on the draft radar to a senior who was a potential first-round pick, to a certain lottery (top 13) pick. Now Thomason and his coaches saw an opportunity for Olowokandi to rise all the way to No. 1 and they were eager to assist him. During workouts following the Tigers' season, the coaches helped Olowokandi get himself into the best shape of his life, adding muscle and some bulk to his already imposing frame. Verlin worked with him relentlessly at least four days a week, using a shield bag, trying to bang Olowokandi inside the paint and throw him off balance. Verlin had always been able to knock Olowokandi around in these drills. No longer. "It got to the point where I had no chance," Verlin recalls now. "He was so big and so strong, he could kill you."

By the time draft week arrived, Olowokandi had already wowed several NBA teams during private workouts, including two for the benefit of the Los Angeles Clippers, who owned the No. 1 pick. Up until then, Arizona point guard Mike Bibby had been considered a virtual lock to go first overall, but sentiment was clearly swinging toward Olowokandi. Conventional wisdom was that no team — particularly not the sad-sack Clips — could afford to pass on an athletic seven-footer with so much of what pro scouts liked to refer to as "upside." Because of his size, athleticism, birthplace and 92-inch wingspan, Olowokandi was drawing favourable comparisons to NBA superstar Hakeem

Olajuwon. "When he came in and worked out, it was amazing the improvement he had shown since the end of the (college) season," Clippers vice-president Elgin Baylor told ESPN. "We knew he had the mentality to play in this league, but until that day we weren't sure he had the tools."

During draft week in Vancouver, British Columbia, rumours abounded, many of them involving Olowokandi. Among the countless questions he was asked was how he would feel about going No. 2 to the Vancouver Grizzlies. "Whatever happens," he replied, "I'll embrace it." The Grizzlies weren't to be in his future, however. Olowokandi had so impressed the Clippers, both with his workouts and his psychological testing, that he was their man. On the morning of the draft, agent Bill Duffy told his client that the Clippers had decided to select him as No. 1. Olowokandi still couldn't believe it. Backstage in the Green Room at General Motors Place, the five minutes the Clippers were alloted to decide upon their top pick seemed to drag on for five hours. Finally, NBA commissioner David Stern stepped up to the podium: "With the first pick in the 1998 NBA draft, the Los Angeles Clippers select Michael Olowokandi from the University of the Pacific."

And there it was: Michael Olowokandi's transformation from raw foreign project to No. 1 NBA draft pick was complete. His amazing journey was over, and a new one was just beginning. "Getting up there and seeing my name at the No. 1 spot — it's unbelievable, especially when you consider where I came from about three years ago," a delighted Olowokandi told reporters afterward. "Not the No. 3 pick, but the No. 1 pick. That's something that will probably take me a week or so, or a little bit longer than that, to get over and embark on my new journey."

Only a week after Olowokandi donned his blue Clippers cap, the NBA and its players descended into the labour lockout that would nearly scuttle an entire season. Olowokandi was a No. 1 pick with no league to play in. Still, he wasn't about to sit around and wait to collect his newfound riches. Olowokandi attended the Pete Newell camp for the second straight summer and embarked on a serious weight-lifting regimen. He worked out individually with former Los Angeles Lakers great Kareem Abdul-Jabbar, who gave him inside tips, and former Clipper Kiki Vandeweghe, who helped him with free-throws and his outside game. He wanted to be ready for his career, whenever it resumed. "I've got this far by working hard and the only way I know how to get better is by working even harder, to try to work to exhaustion," he told ESPN after the draft. "I'm not so stupid that I'd take this for granted."

Olowokandi would have to wait until February 1998, nearly eight months later, to play his first NBA game and start collecting his four-year, $12-million U.S. contract. In the meantime, he signed with Kinder Bologna of the Italian League and played a rather forgettable professional stint in Europe, averaging 7.7 points, 5.8 rebounds and 14 minutes over six games. By the time he was released to join the Clips, he had missed most of his first NBA training camp and was thrown into a hellish, abbreviated season with a long-struggling franchise. Not exactly prime conditions for a young player, particularly a player so new to the game as Olowokandi.

"He came into the league under the most extenuating circumstances of any No. 1 pick in the history of the league, I believe," says Clippers head coach Chris Ford. "Without question, everything's a lesson for him." The lessons haven't been easy. While other top rookies from his class — Vince Carter of Toronto, Sacramento's

Jason Williams and Mike Bibby of Vancouver — stepped in and become major forces in their first year, Olowokandi's progress has been slower. He led all rookies in rebounding with 7.9 boards per game but his 8.9 points per contest could have been much higher had his shooting percentage (.431) and free-throw percentage (.483) been better. In a preview of things to come, Olowokandi averaged more than a block a game for the Clippers, who again struggled mightily, finishing with a 9–41 record, second-worst only to the Grizzlies.

The best overall statistical effort of Olowokandi's rookie season came on April 21, 1999, in Vancouver, when he made a 16-point, 17-rebound, three-steal night look easy. But afterward, he certainly didn't sound overly impressed with himself. "Every time you come in and have a good individual game, it always gives you a good feeling," he said after a disappointing 97–94 loss to the Grizzlies. "But when I came here tonight I didn't have any goals or any plans to grab 17 rebounds or come out with a career high. I came here to win. There is no consolation in (individual statistics) for me, unfortunately."

Olowokandi's progress as a rookie seems to have satisfied the Clippers, who are counting on the kind of growth that occurred during his time at Pacific. But at least one major publication gave Olowokandi's rookie season the thumbs down. In May 1999, *The Sporting News* tabbed Olowokandi as 1998's worst first-round draft pick. His first NBA coach, a man who could often be spotted yelling personal instructions to Olowokandi from the bench throughout his rookie season, was far more generous with his evaluation. "He's coming along," Ford said, late in Olowokandi's first NBA campaign. "The experience factor — there's an enormous difference between him and other guys who've played growing up and played all throughout their lives. But he's also a little stubborn at times. He's got to realize that I have a wealth of experience playing the game, being around the game and he's got to be patient enough to listen to us as well."

If his track record at Pacific is any indication, Olowokandi will listen and absorb his lessons. But the NBA is, to use his own words, more "plurally dimensional." Players are often responsible for defending much more than their own man. There is a 24-second shot clock to consider, leaving less time for decisions on the court. There are more games and there is more pressure. "There's a whole lot more to deal with," Olowokandi admits. One of those "things" is the media. And with Olowokandi, there is an added dimension of responsibility. He is not only a No. 1 draft pick, he has also become an icon for basketball-playing kids in England. As such, his story is followed in the country he still considers home. "Sports like rugby or soccer are pretty much what people are into back there," says Olowokandi, who returns to England every summer. Nevertheless, there was enough European interest in Olowokandi's rookie NBA season to make him the lone subject of a February conference call with British reporters. During that session, Olowokandi was asked by a British journalist whether, as an NBA player in Los Angeles, he was inundated by fans. "It's not to the point where girls are chasing me down the street like the Beatles or anything," he laughed. Olowokandi's advice to kids in Britain who wish to follow in his size-18 footsteps is to work hard, try to minimize the weaknesses in your game and believe in your dreams.

A strong belief in himself will certainly help Olowokandi to continue to learn his lessons in the NBA. "I know for a fact that every day I come in, I learn something new," Olowokandi says. "I feel more comfortable and that happens each and every game and I hope that continues to happen. I don't know if I've reached the point where I'm completely comfortable, where I feel I can go out there and put a team on my back or go out there and pretty much be confident we'll come out with a victory based on my effort alone. It was a little bit different in college. I think I got to a point where I could do that, and that would be my goal in the pros — however long that might take."

At this point, Olowokandi might seem far removed from that goal. But considering where he has come from, the distance isn't so daunting. "I think he's going to be very good," says Verlin, the Pacific big-man coach who spent so many hours in the gym working with Olowokandi. "I think you're going to see a big-time improvement in the next two years. I mean, this is only his fourth year of basketball."

Those four years have been a crash course in a new sport and a new way of life. It's a course that might not have been possible had Tony Marcopulos not been around to answer that phone in the Pacific basketball office back on April 3, 1995. Olowokandi's path would have been far different — and who knows if he'd even be in the NBA now? Even to its protagonist, who has told it over and over again, it is still an amazing story. "It is," Olowokandi admits. "But I usually try to just move on and do what I have to do right now. It's not the time to cherish my accomplishments. That'll happen when I retire. Right now I have a lot of work and a lot of things ahead of me that I'm trying to accomplish and I'll try to focus on that."

One thing is certain: Pacific was a good place for Michael Olowokandi to land. Fate brought him together with the relatively small Northern California university and the result has been a storyline so compelling that it has attracted interest from the heavyweight Hollywood company DreamWorks. "The odds were literally one in a million," Marcopulos says. "It'll never happen again. I couldn't even make this story up." The relationship between Pacific and Michael Olowokandi was mutually beneficial. He developed into a No. 1 pick and the school reaped the rewards, both on the court and in the recruiting process. Nowadays, an aspiring big man will look at Pacific a little more favourably when trying to decide on a school.

"We got him the ball in a million ways," Pacific head coach Bob Thomason says. "At a bigger school, he might not have played. How patient would North Carolina have been? Michael could have got lost in the shuffle in a bigger school. This was a perfect situation for him."

"I don't think he would have ever been the first pick in the draft if he hadn't been at Pacific," Marcopulos adds.

The final two seasons that Pacific experienced with Olowokandi in the middle have been the best of Thomason's coaching career. He is thankful that fate conspired to match up the Kandi Man with his school and his program. "I think it's an unbelievable story," Thomason says. "I don't think it will ever happen again. It's just something that happened here. And everyone got to enjoy it."

ESSENTIAL OLOWOKANDI

Name: Michael Olowokandi (pronounced "O-Lo-Wah-Can-Dee")
Nickname: "The Kandi Man"
Position: Centre, Los Angeles Clippers
Born: April 3, 1975; Lagos, Nigeria
Height: 7'   **Weight:** 269 lbs.
High school: Newlands Manor School, East Sussex, England
U.S. college: University of the Pacific, Stockton, CA
Drafted: 1998, No. 1 overall by Los Angeles Clippers

COLLEGE
As a sophomore (1995–96)
25 games; 257 total minutes; .526 from field; 0 from three-point range; .556 from free-throw line; 84 total rebounds; 3.4 rebounds per game; 14 total assists; 0.2 assists per game; 100 total points; 4.0 points per game.

As a junior (1996–97)
19 games; 433 total minutes; .570 from field; 0 from three-point range; .333 from free-throw line; 126 total rebounds; 6.6 rebounds per game; 8 total assists; 0.4 assists per game; 207 total points; 10.9 points per game.

As a senior (1997–98)
33 games; 1,046 total minutes; .608 from field; 0 from three-point range; .485 from free-throw line; 369 total rebounds; 11.2 rebounds per game; 26 total assists; 0.8 assists per game; 732 total points; 22.2 points per game.

College career (1995–98)
77 games; 1,736 total minutes; .591 from field; none from three-point range; .466 from free-throw line; 579 total rebounds; 7.5 rebounds per game; 38 assists; 0.5 assists per game; 1,039 total points; 13.5 points per game.

College honours
1997-98 — Big West Conference Player of the Year; Associated Press honorable mention All-America selection; conference record five-time Big West Player of the week.

College records
Pacific record for most career blocks (160), most single-season blocks (95), most points in single season (732), career field goal

percentage (.591), and single-season field goal percentage (.608).

NBA
1998–99 (Clippers)
45 games; 36 games started; 1,279 total minutes; 28.4 minutes per game; .431 from field; none from three-point range; .483 from free-throw line; 357 total rebounds; 7.9 rebounds per game; 25 total assists; 0.6 assists per game; 55 blocks; 27 steals; 401 total points; 8.9 points per game.

NBA honours
1998–99 — NBA All-Rookie Second Team.

Sources
Sports Illustrated feature, Sept. 14, 1998

Associated Press

Canadian Press

Vancouver *Sun*

Vancouver *Province*

Los Angeles *Daily News*

ESPN

The Sporting News

University of the Pacific men's basketball website

NBA.com

Official NBA Register, (regular-season) Guide and Draft Media Guide

DAWN STALEY

It wasn't easy to fit in, at least not right away. For one thing, Dawn Staley was usually the only girl looking for a spot in the pickup basketball games in her rough-and-tumble North Philadelphia neighbourhood. For another, she wasn't exactly big for her age.

At first, she used her own basketball as bait. "You can't use my ball if I can't play," the pre-teen Dawn would tell the young boys who were reluctant to have a girl join their game. Later, as she graduated to games with teenagers and young men, she solved the problem in a different manner. "Playing on the playgrounds and in the community centres with the guys definitely contributed to my style of play," Staley says now. "I had a lot of trouble getting my shot off because I was a lot shorter than most of the guys. So I worked on passing the basketball. And it became a passion." And the rest, one might say, is hoops history.

Since those earliest days of dribbling and dreaming, Dawn Staley has evolved into the unofficial princess of the pass. Now a dynamic five-foot-six point guard with the Charlotte Sting of the Women's National Basketball Association (WNBA), she has been labelled the "Magic Johnson" of women's basketball by no less an authority than Magic himself. But that deep desire to distribute the ball began back on those North Philly courts, out of necessity and a simple, burning love for the intricate beauty of the team game. It began out of a passion for the pass.

It wasn't easy for a female to step into the games that were played in Staley's neighbourhood. She grew up with three brothers and one sister in the Raymond Rosen housing projects, a tough area of North Philadelphia where money was often short and the basketball games at the Moylan recreation center stretched long into the night. But before she left her hometown for college and later the pros, Staley had become a star fixture in the same city that produced hoops legend Wilt Chamberlain.

The inner-city setting in which she grew up was poor, but Staley never went without. Her mother, Estelle, made sure of that. Dawn's wants were pretty simple. A decent pair of sneakers was usually all she needed to be happy. And there was never a shortage of motivation or competition in her surroundings. "In the neighbourhood I grew up in, people (tended) to write us off," Staley says. "They didn't give us an opportunity. That's what motivated me to want to do things. I wanted to prove people wrong. Definitely, the neighbourhood I grew up in, I wouldn't change for the world. It has made me the player and the person I am today." Those surroundings allowed Dawn Staley to discover pretty quickly that she was naturally gifted with a basketball and that she harboured a deep love for the game. She played every day, winter and summer, and she never, ever, tired of it. "I still love the game," she says now, the commitment ringing true in her voice. "I wouldn't play it if I didn't."

Staley came by her love of basketball honestly. In Philadelphia, the NBA's 76ers ruled the sports scene in the early 1980s. The beloved Sixers reached the NBA

finals three times, winning a league championship during a memorable 1982–83 season. Like so many other
youngsters pounding the city's outdoor courts, Dawn
Staley worshipped the play of classy Philadelphia point
guard Maurice Cheeks, a four-time all-star who kept
the game simple and got the job done with amazing
efficiency. And like so many others, Staley dreamed of
following in Cheeks' footsteps, all the way to the NBA.
But unlike most of those other dreamers in the City of
Brotherly Love, Staley was a sister. "I always had aspira-
tions of actually playing in the NBA," she says now. "I
believed I could, but reality — that's a different picture.
Women's basketball was something that wasn't on TV
then and you never heard a lot about it. The only wom-
en's game I had ever watched (as a youngster) was one
NCAA championship game. I saw that game and it was
like: 'I can play with them' even though my sister told
me I couldn't."

It wouldn't be long before Staley would prove her
point to her doubting sister — and everybody else. But
first she had to hone her game against the guys, and
that wasn't always easy. Despite the fact she could hold
her own against most of the young men she played, she
met up with a lot of early resistance and not a few cat-
calls, often hearing disparaging comments like "put a
skirt on" or "go back to the kitchen." Looking back on
it now, it was intimidating. "Very much so," Staley admits. "You didn't know how they were going to take
you. It took a while to get accepted. But I was just really
persistent and I earned my keep. Creating chances for
the bigger guys — that was one way to earn your spot."

Creating chances. That's what Staley's game has always been about — that and entertainment. From the
day she first stepped onto the blacktop and fearlessly
proved herself against the bigger, stronger boys, she was

aware she had a certain flair for the game. She could set people up to score and she could do so in style. That flair was evident by the time Staley reached Dobbins Technical to embark on one of the finest high-school careers in Philadelphia prep hoops history.

"When Dawn came to our school, she brought new life into the team," recalls Rich Yankowitz, who has been a boys' basketball coach at Dobbins for 28 years and who had a front row seat for the Staley era. "When she went onto that court, she brought excitement to the game immediately."

Dawn Staley brought star power to Dobbins girls' basketball — power contained in a five-and-a-half-foot package. Not only could she score like few other prep players, she also kept all four of her teammates on the court deeply involved through her playmaking. By then she had long recognized that being a good passer is all about knowing your teammates' strengths and weaknesses, knowing where they like to receive the ball, both on the break and in the half-court game. She knew that by accounting for her teammates' abilities, she could make it easier on them with her passes. As a result, everybody loved playing with her.

Prep success came fast and furious under Staley's creative, generous style of leadership. She would steer Dobbins to three straight Philadelphia Public League titles — the competitive pinnacle for girl's basketball teams in the Philly high schools, which don't compete in state playoffs. Dobbins won city championships in Staley's sophomore, junior and senior seasons. Staley's high school exploits at Dobbins earned her a city-wide notoriety and the attention of college coaches across the country. But Yankowitz says her development was a result of things well beyond what was happening in the Dobbins gym. "She was a talent before she got to high school," he says. "She was the player that she was because she didn't practise just with the team. She played constantly in the schoolyards, she played with the fellas. She didn't really play too much with the girls … If a girl has a lot of talent, she's not going to get the push — the competitive edge — (just) playing against other girls."

Despite the superior skills, athleticism and on-court intelligence that separated her from the pack, Staley was popular at Dobbins, with both teachers and fellow students. Yankowitz says she was never "stuck on herself." In fact, he recalls her as shy, a near honour-roll student who kept her head down and sometimes had trouble looking people in the eye. Until she got on the court, that is. Then she shone like no other player. "Everyone knew she was something special," Yankowitz recalls. "She was out of the ordinary — a godsend."

Dawn Staley's on-court exploits meant that, despite her relatively diminutive stature, she was becoming one of the hottest high school recruits of her era. She could have gone to any college in the U.S., but it was the University of Virginia that would ultimately win the battle for her services. Virginia had been interested in Staley ever since she was an eighth-grade wunderkind. Fittingly, however, it was actually a North Philadelphia playground game at which University of Virginia Cavaliers' head coach Debbie Ryan first discovered her future point guard. Shortly after that first encounter, coach Ryan wrote Staley a letter — the only contact permissible for players that young under the NCAA's strict recruiting rules. "She always remembered that letter," Ryan says now.

Both Penn State and Iowa also made serious pitches that Staley considered before making her decision. But after taking a visit to Virginia's Charlottesville campus, Staley felt comfortable there. She liked the dorm rooms, the academic challenges and the fact that Virginia was relatively close to her friends and family back in Philadelphia. She committed to a full scholarship with the Cavaliers a day before the end of the NCAA signing period. "Virginia was just a good fit for her," Ryan says.

At the time, Debbie Ryan was already well on her way to becoming one of the NCAA's most respected and successful women's basketball coaches. She had been the head coach at Virginia since 1978 when she endured an 8–17 season in her first winter on the bench. But that was the only losing season Ryan would experience. She steadily built up the Cavaliers program and, as with any college team, good recruiting was important to Virginia's rise. No recruit would be more crucial to Ryan's team than Dawn Staley.

Ryan remembers the pint-sized point guard from Philadelphia who showed up on campus in the fall of 1988 as a study in contrasts. Off the court, the freshman was extremely quiet and kept to herself. But on the hardwood, she was expressive in a manner few players have the game to back up. "She had a lot of mustard," Ryan laughs. "Dawn had incredible court vision at a very young age." That vision would help transform the Virginia program into a women's basketball powerhouse during Staley's four years at the school. The Cavaliers went 21–10 overall and muddled their way to an 8–6 Atlantic Coast Conference (ACC) record during her freshman season, with Staley leading the team in scoring at 18.5 points per game. That was merely a taste, however, of what was to come.

Dawn Staley would go on to lead the Cavaliers into three consecutive Final Fours in her final three seasons. Her infectious, entertaining style would also help to popularize women's college basketball across the U.S. and especially at Virginia, where the Cavaliers sold out the 8,457-seat University Hall on some nights. "She had a very good work ethic. She was always a great example for everybody," Ryan says of the impact Staley had on her program. "We had a lot of good players during the time she was here, but Dawn was the key."

The only goal Staley didn't achieve at Virginia was an NCAA championship. Her Cavaliers came awfully close — in 1991 they lost a 70–67 overtime heartbreaker to Tennessee in the championship game and they reached the NCAA semifinals in 1990 and 1992, losing to Stanford both times by a combined total of 10 points. At the same time, Staley piled up a trophy room full of personal awards, including Final Four MVP in 1991, three straight Kodak All-America awards and back-to-back Champion, U.S. Basketball Writers Association (USBWA) and Naismith national Player of the Year honours. In 1991, she was also named winner of the Honda-Broderick Cup, awarded annually to the nation's outstanding female collegiate athlete in any sport. As one of only three Virginia players to have her number (24) retired, Staley also left her mark statistically. She finished her career at Virginia as the NCAA's all-time steals leader (454) and the only player in Atlantic Coast Conference history to post a combination of more than 2,000 points, 700 rebounds, 700 assists and 400 steals. Almost unbelievably, considering her five-foot-six stature, Staley is still fifth on Virginia's career rebounding list (772) and eighth on the Cavaliers' all-time blocked shots list (52). She remains the school's all-time leading scorer and the only Cavalier player to ever post a triple-double. All of this came from a player who surrendered half a foot — or more — in height to many of the top collegiate players. But Staley's lack of size has never seemed to be a factor. "She never let it be," Ryan says. "Dawn is always looking to improve or to do better. I think she's always looking for an advantage. She has a passion for the game and a desire to do something significant with her life."

Perhaps the most telling statistic about Staley's career at Virginia is the fact that her scoring average actually decreased each year she was in college while her assists total climbed dramatically. Not coincidentally, team victories also rose to unprecedented heights. Dawn Staley didn't win a national championship at Virginia, but she did realize her other major goal entering the school. In May of 1992, she graduated with a degree in Rhetoric and Communications Studies.

Debbie Ryan is probably a little biased, but in 22 years as an NCAA women's basketball head coach, she has never seen another point guard like Staley. "I definitely think she was the best ever," Ryan says. "But as good a player as Dawn is, she's an even better person. She's very giving, very unselfish. I've never seen another college player like her. She was special to the game."

Following her outstanding college career at Virginia, Staley went on to play professionally in Brazil, France, Italy and Spain before returning to North America to spend two seasons in the now-defunct American Basketball League (ABL), a former rival to the WNBA. The ABL played in the traditional winter season and many observers felt it offered a superior brand of basketball. Playing with the Richmond Rage out of Richmond, Virginia, Staley led the entire ABL in assists with eight per game and averaged 14.9 points as she steered her team into the league finals in 1996–97. That season she finished third in MVP balloting for the ABL.

In her second and final ABL season, Staley got the opportunity to return home to Philadelphia when the Richmond franchise relocated. She led the Rage with 13.2 points and 6.5 assists a game and became a certified hometown hoops hero. In fact, Staley was the subject of a gigantic, seven-storey mural that, even after the team was gone, graced an office building on the corner of Eighth and Market in downtown Philly. Seeing her likeness a half-dozen storeys high is a feeling Staley can describe only as "overwhelming."

After the 1997-98 season, Staley made the decision to jump to the WNBA, a league backed by the NBA with a higher profile and a summer-only schedule. The move was positive in two major ways — Staley would get better exposure as a basketball player and her knees would take less of a pounding because she would be playing fewer games per year. Not long after Staley announced she was jumping to the WNBA, the ABL folded.

Like most other ABL players, Staley was placed into a draft pool for selection in May of 1999. She was chosen ninth overall by the Charlotte Sting, a team looking for a point guard and precisely the kind of set-up skills in which Staley specializes. For Charlotte coach Marynell Meadors, the arrival of Dawn Staley was a reason to celebrate. Her club, which had made the WNBA's Final Four the previous season, was now getting the court quarterback it lacked. The Sting head coach couldn't believe that Staley was still around at No. 9 on a draft day that had been dominated by the No. 1 overall selection of University of Tennessee superstar Chamique Holdsclaw. After going through her first two seasons in Charlotte with fresh-out-of-college rookies Tora Suber and Christy Smith running the Sting offence, Meadors was pleased to have a veteran like Staley at the controls, somebody who could consistently get the ball to Sting scoring threats Andrea Stinson, Vicky Bullett and Tracy Reid. "I think we got a true point guard in Dawn Staley," Meadors told the North American media in a WNBA coaches' pre-season conference call. "I mean, there's no question about it, what she's brought to our team has been leadership."

Staley's giving nature and leadership qualities certainly shone during one of her first public functions as a member of the Charlotte Sting. During a WNBA Internet chat with fans, Staley was asked a few questions by young women to whom she is obviously an idol. "I am a 13-year-old female and I play basketball," wrote one fan from the Bronx. "I am a good player but what separates me from the other girls is my weight. It shows in games on defence and in practice when running laps or sprints. People tell me there's no way I'm going to be skinny because my family is big. I don't want to be skinny but just slim. What should I do?"

Replied Dawn: "First of all, be proud of who you are and all the gifts God has given to you. Size is a factor in basketball only if you make it that way. Eat healthy, stay strong and keep a good positive attitude. Keep working hard to improve the weaker parts of your game. If you're not as fast as other players, work on your footwork, your positioning on the floor and moving without the basketball."

Asked another fan, a young girl from California: "If you want to play basketball, but you don't think that you are as good as the other girls, then what should you do?"

Dawn: "Practise, practise, practise … and maybe not think so much."

Staley's WNBA team struggled to begin the 1999 season, going 5–7 and prompting the club to fire head coach and General Manager Marynell Meadors after just 12 games. Meadors was replaced by assistant coach Dan Hughes. Dawn averaged 11.5 points and 5.5 assists (third best in the league) to help the Sting reach the Eastern Conference finals.

For Staley, the WNBA is just the latest chapter in the basketball journey that began on the North Philly blacktop 20 years ago. "I'm just hoping to help raise the level of women's professional basketball," Staley says of her goals in the WNBA. "I hope to bring entertainment to it. And I want to let young women know that they can realize a dream. I've experienced the whole spectrum of women's basketball and it's long overdue," she adds of the attention the WNBA is now receiving. "We deserve that."

Dawn Staley's biggest basketball dream to date wasn't realized in a high school, college or professional uniform, however. Instead it came in the red-white-and-blue colours of her nation. When she helped steer the U.S. to the gold medal at the 1996 Olympics, it was the greatest accomplishment of her career. In fact, Staley has long been a key figure for USA Basketball's national-team program, helping the U.S. to the 1994 Goodwill Games championship, for which she was named USA Basketball's Female Athlete of the Year. She was also a member of the U.S. team which won the world championship in 1998 and she figures to play an important international role in the next Olympics as she is part of a core of six players who have been pre-selected for the team that will compete in the 2000 Games at Sydney, Australia.

Wherever she goes, and at whatever level she is playing, Staley will always be known as the ultimate court quarterback, a player who improves everybody around her and infects them with her own deep love of the game. That unselfishness comes across easily on the basketball court, where Dawn Staley still piles up the assists, and in interviews, where she gives freely of herself to strangers. It also comes across in her recent work off the bas-ketball court. Like an increasing number of high-profile pro athletes, she has established an organization to reach out to her community. The non-profit Dawn Staley Foundation helps at-risk youth by offering after-school programs, scholarships and a community basketball league in Philadelphia. In 1998, Staley was recognized for her community work with the American Red Cross Spectrum Award, which honours women who have made a significant contribution to their communities.

"Dawn Staley reminds me of myself," the legendary Magic Johnson said in a *Hoop* magazine feature on Staley in February of 1999. "She's the Lady Magic Johnson. Like other great players, Dawn makes everyone play better on the court."

Staley has practically become a legend herself. She was recently named by the Philadelphia *Daily News* as the city's greatest female athlete of the century. To all those kids in Philly — and especially to the girls — she is a beacon, an example who shows youngsters that if you want something badly enough, you can go get it. You don't need to be seven feet tall or male. You just need the desire.

Twenty-odd years ago, Dawn Staley began chasing her dream. She started out on a playground with a pair of sneakers, a ball and an attitude that eventually convinced the doubters she wasn't going to be denied. Staley still looks back at those days in North Philly as the biggest reason she is where she is today. "I'm still close to some of the guys I grew up playing with (in Philly)," she laughs. "They have a special place in my heart."

STALEY STUFF

Name: Dawn Michelle Staley
Born: May 4, 1970; Philadelphia, PA
Height: 5'6"   **Weight:** 134 lbs.
Position: Point guard, Charlotte Sting
High School: Dobbins Technical, North Philadelphia, PA
College: University of Virginia, Charlottesville, VA
Drafted: 1999, No. 9 overall by the Charlotte Sting

COLLEGE

As a freshman (1988–89)
31 games; .457 from field; .355 from three-point range; .831 from free-throw line; 158 total rebounds; 5.1 rebounds per game; 144 total assists; 4.6 assists per game; 574 total points; 18.5 points per game.

As a sophomore (1989–90)
32 games; .452 from field; .346 from three-point range; .781 from free-throw line; 214 total rebounds; 6.7 rebounds per game; 141 total assists; 4.4 assists per game; 574 total points; 17.9 points per game.

As a junior (1990–91)
34 games; .450 from field; .324 from three-point range; .824 from free-throw line; 209 total rebounds; 6.1 rebounds per game; 235 total assists; 6.9 assists per game; 495 total points; 14.6 points per game.

As a senior (1991–92)
34 games; .484 from field; .303 from three-point range; .808 from free-throw line; 181 total rebounds; 5.6 rebounds per game; 209 total assists; 6.1 assists per game; 492 total points; 14.5 points per game.

College career (1988–92)
131 games; .460 from field; .334 from three-point range; .811 from free-throw line; 772 total rebounds; 5.9 rebounds per game; 729 total assists; 5.6 assists per game; 454 steals; 2,135 total points; 16.3 points per game.

College honours
1991 — Honda-Broderick Cup award (Collegiate Woman Athlete of the Year); *Sports Illustrated* Player of the Year; Honda Basketball Sports Award Winner; Outstanding Philadelphia

Amateur Athlete (Philadelphia Sports Writers Association);
NCAA Final Four All-Tournament selection; 1991 Final Four
Outstanding Player.

1991 and 1992 — Champion USA Player of Year; Women's
Basketball Coaches Association (WBCA) Player of the Year;
Naismith Player of the Year; U.S. Basketball Writers Association
Player of the Year; Atlantic Coast Conference Player of the Year;
NCAA Final Four All-Tournament selection.

All-America Honours — U.S. Basketball Writers Association
(USBWA) (twice); Kodak All-American (three times).

College records

NCAA total steals in a career (454); only player (male or
female) in ACC history to have a combination of more than
2,000 points, 700 rebounds, 700 assists and 400 steals;
Virginia and ACC total assists (729); Virginia career scoring
average (16.3 points per game).

ABL; WNBA
1996–97 (Richmond Rage, ABL)
40 games; .402 from field; .314 from three-point range; .832
from free-throw line; 147 total rebounds; 3.7 rebounds per
game; 320 total assists; 8.0 assists per game; 111 steals; 597
total points; 14.9 points per game.
1997–98 (Philadelphia Rage, ABL)
41 games; .395 from field; .389 from three-point range; .837
from free-throw line; 133 total rebounds; 3.2 rebounds per
game; 266 total assists; 6.5 assists per game; 535 total points;
13.2 points per game.
ABL career totals (1996–98)
81 games; .398 from field; .366 from three-point range; .833
from free-throw line; 280 total rebounds; 3.5 rebounds per
game; 586 total assists; 7.2 assists per game; 1,132 total points;
14.0 points per game.
1998–99 (Charlotte Sting, WNBA)
32 games; 32 games started; 1065 total minutes; 33.3 minutes
per game; .415 from field; .317 from three-point range; .934
from free-throw line; 72 total rebounds; 2.3 rebounds per game;
177 total assists; 5.5 assists per game; 3 blocks; 38 steals; 368
total points; 11.5 points per game.

Playoffs to date (1999)

4 games; 4 started; 157 total minutes; 39.3 minutes per game; .325 from field; .438 from three-point range; .833 from free-throw line; 5 total rebounds; 1.3 rebounds per game; 23 total assists; 5.8 assists per game; 0 blocks; 3 steals; 48 total points; 12 points per game.

ABL honours

1996–97 — started in ABL All-Star Game; led ABL in assists; third in 1996-97 ABL MVP voting; All-ABL first team.
1997–98 — started in ABL All-Star Game; All-ABL second team.

Olympic honours

1996 — Atlanta Olympic Games (U.S. gold-medal winning team)

International honours

1994 — USA Basketball Female Athlete of the Year.
1994 — MVP, 1994 Goodwill Games and member of championship team.
1998 — Member of U.S. women's world championship team.

Sources

Hoop Magazine feature, February, 1999
Associated Press
Official WNBA Guide and Register
WNBA.com
University of Virginia women's basketball website

JEFF RUD is a sports columnist with the Victoria *Times-Colonist* and the author of the critically acclaimed book *Long Shot: Steve Nash's Journey to the NBA* (Polestar, 1996). He has covered basketball for *USA Today* and the CBC Television program *The Score*. Jeff lives and works in Victoria, British Columbia.

BRIGHT LIGHTS FROM POLESTAR BOOK PUBLISHERS

Polestar takes pride in creating books that enrich our understanding of the world and introduce discriminating readers to exciting writers. Here are some of our best-selling sports titles.

Long Shot: Steve Nash's Journey to the NBA *by Jeff Rud*
Profile of young NBA star Steve Nash, detailing the determination and skill that carried him through high school and college basketball into the ranks of the pros.
1-896095-16-x • $18.95 CDN/$16.95 USA

Celebrating Excellence: Canadian Women Athletes *by Wendy Long*
A collection of biographical essays and photos that showcases more than 200 female athletes who have achieved excellence.
1-896095-04-6 • $29.95 CDN/$24.95 USA

Our Game: A Collection of All-Star Hockey Fiction
by Doug Beardsley, editor
From the Forum to the backyard rink, this collection of 30 stories illuminates the essence of the hockey soul.
1-896095-26-7 • $18.95 CDN/$16.95 USA

Behind the Mask, revised edition *by Ian Young and Chris Gudgeon*
Here is every goaltender's essential handbook, including physical and psychological techniques and game-action photos.
1-896095-51-8 • $18.95 CDN/$14.95 USA

Home Run: A Modern Approach to Baseball Skill Building
by Michael McRae
Skills specialist McRae offers a solid base of technical instruction for players and coaches who are learning and teaching baseball fundamentals.
1-896095-29-1 • $18.95 CDN/$15.95 USA

Too Many Men on the Ice: Women's Hockey in North America
by Joanna Avery and Julie Stevens
A fascinating look at all levels of women's hockey in Canada and the United States, including in-depth profiles of prominent players.
1-896095-33-X • $19.95 CDN/$16.95 USA

Polestar titles are available from your local bookseller.
For a copy of our catalogue, contact:
POLESTAR BOOK PUBLISHERS
103-1014 Homer Street
Vancouver, BC
Canada   V6B 2W9
polestar@direct.ca